W9-AOO-379

THE WORLD IS LEARNING
COMPASSION

FRANK C. LAUBACH

The World
Is Learning
Compassion

FLEMING H. REVELL COMPANY

FLEMING H. REVELL COMPANY

Westwood, New Jersey

London E. C. 4—29 Ludgate Hill

Glasgow C. 2—229 Bothwell Street

FOREWORD

THE PURPOSE OF THIS BOOK IS TO SHOW THAT THE COMPASSION of Jesus, which has been kept alive for nineteen centuries within the Christian church, has in this century burst out into the secular realm. It is well on the way to becoming the creed and practice of the world.

Volumes could be written, and have been written, about the compassion of Christ within the Christian church; that is to be expected. The church ceases to be the church when the compassion of Christ does not flow through it.

But the new thing, the wonderful thing, the world-transforming thing, is that the compassion of Jesus has broken all bounds, and is now revolutionizing the attitude of the whole world toward the underprivileged multitudes. They are no longer merely "cheap labor" to be exploited for profit. They are human beings, souls, to be helped up into the abundant life.

The fact that two-thirds of the human race lives in miserable poverty is not new. It is as old as the human race. The new thing is that both the people who *have* and the people who *have not* are really trying to do something to wipe out that poverty and misery.

THAT IS NEW! It is not new for genuine Christians, but it is new as a world philosophy and a world deed. And it is the most amazing fact of our era. It is reaching out to change the whole planet.

This book tells how.

CONTENTS

8 CONTENTS

THE WORLD IS LEARNING
COMPASSION

CHAPTER 1

A VOICE FROM THE DEPTHS

WHEN MY WIFE AND I WENT TO THE ISLAND OF MINDANAO IN THE southern Philippines in 1915, we little dreamed that our literacy experiments there would ultimately take us to six continents and ninety-one countries to help educators prepare literacy textbooks in 262 languages. Our guiding principle was: "Nobody knows whether a lesson is right but the illiterate. If it works, it is right." So we have sat down beside tens of thousands of illiterates all over the world to test these lessons. This globe-trotting among the underprivileged people has enabled us to take a "worm's-eye view" of the world and its problems. We can look up from the depths with the eyes and the emotions of our illiterate friends at you more fortunate people above. Year after year we have been returning from those depths to plead in America and Europe for understanding and assistance. We have lived forty-one years among them, and thirty-one years among you. We feel God's call to be their interpreter and spokesmen.

"Three out of five of the human race cannot read or write."

This was the startling revelation made in 1927 by James F. Abel, of the United States Bureau of Education. In the conti-

11

nents of Asia and Africa alone, over a billion people are illiterate, *eight persons out of every ten,* half of the human race! This cold type cannot tell you what that means.

You think it is a pity they cannot read.

The real tragedy is that they have no voice in public affairs, they never vote, they are never represented in any conference. They have been the silent victims, the forgotten men, driven like animals, mutely submitting in every age before and since the pyramids.

It is a human weakness not to become aware of suffering unless we hear a cry. This illiterate majority of the human race does not know how to reach us with its cry. Hence we never know how they suffer.

The most bruised people on this planet, the naked, the hungry, the fallen-among-thieves, the sick, the imprisoned in mind and soul, are the twelve hundred million adult illiterates. At least *a billion of them are virtually slaves!* Almost every illiterate is in debt all his life, and his children, and his children's children inherit the debt. He does not know how much his debt is, nor whether the interest on it is correct. The moneylender takes all he can take and still keep his victim alive; it would be silly for him to kill the animal that makes him rich. In one form or another, this is the black sorrow of nearly every illiterate in the world.

More than half the human race is hungry, driven, diseased, afraid of educated men in this world and of demons in the next one.

I have seen these people across Asia and Africa and Latin America, and have sat beside them to teach them one by one. I have seen a new light kindle in their eyes; I have seen love and hope in their faces as they stepped out of blindness and began to read. I know that we could free this multitude from their tragic bondage; indeed, their emancipation has already begun.

The curve of literacy, which has been nearly stationary in Asia and Africa for centuries, has turned upward recently, especially in the past twenty years. A hundred million more adults read today than read twenty years ago. If that curve follows its present trend, within fifty years we shall have five hundred million readers stepping out of the silent ranks of illiteracy to speak for the first time.

This is not only exciting news. It is the most stupendous, the most arresting, and it may be the most ominous fact on this planet. Nothing can stop it now.[1]

If they could write, this is what the illiterates would say to us:

The Silent Billion Write A Letter

Dear American Friends:

We who belong to the hungry three-fourths of the world are having a great awakening. We are hungry, but we are determined that our children shall not be hungry. We are sick, but we are determined that our children shall not be sick. We are ignorant, but we are determined that our children shall not be ignorant.

A great many millions of us illiterates are hearing the promises of the communists. We want what they promise to give us more than anything else in the world—food, education, health. We don't like to kill people to get what we want. We hate violence. We hate hate. We need what they offer, but we don't like their method.

And yet it is not difficult to stir up hate within us. When wealthy people whirl by us in automobiles while we stand on the roadside hungry, it is hard not to hate. But if an automobile stops and the people in it help us and smile at us, then our hate turns suddenly to love. People tell you sometimes that we are not grateful. Don't believe them. We would die for you, if we knew you were sincere.

Now, to our amazement, you privileged people are reaching your hands down to help us magnificently. You are doing what the communists promise they will do if we kill you. You are sending us food and clothing and medicine. You are helping us to help ourselves out of our poverty and disease.

The communists say this is being done only because you fear *them*. They say you will stop helping us when you are no longer afraid.

Prove that the communists are lying! We want to believe that

[1] Frank C. Laubach, *The Silent Billion Speak* (New York: Friendship Press).

you really are our friends. We want to believe that, more than anything else in the world. Our very lives depend upon your being sincere, upon your meaning it, upon your not trying to fool us because you are afraid of the communists. You don't need to worry about us. We will be your friends. We will stand by you.

But you don't realize how often we have been deceived by educated people; how often a moneylender has loaned us 50 rupees and got our ignorant fingerprint for 500; how many times we have been forced to give up all of our land and all we had, because we were not smart enough to know what was ours legally. We didn't know how to protect ourselves. A billion of us are sharecroppers. You don't realize how the landlord has taken all but a bare subsistence from us for our work. He has no mercy. He has broken our hearts until we don't work as we should, because we are working for robbers. The moneylenders and the landlords are the only educated people we have ever met, except a few missionaries, until recent years.

When, in this amazing fashion, you people far away began to send us shiploads of food, clothing, implements and skilled friends to show us how to make better use of our land and how to get well, it was too good to be true. There must be a joker in it! Whenever men were kind to us in the past, we found later they had an ulterior motive. What motive have you in doing this?

The missionaries say that you learned it from Jesus. They say that is the way He was, and that everybody who really follows Him is like that. They say that He loved people for their own sakes, and that He died defending the poor. If you got this kindness from Jesus, prove it to us. Make us sure that it isn't the other thing, the deception we have always known. Then we will love you. We will work for you. We will die for you. We will love you as nobody ever loved anybody since the world began. Prove that this is real, that it isn't a dream, that it isn't another swindle, the most colossal deception the world ever knew. Prove to us that you are what you seem to be, what the missionaries tell us you

are. If it was really Jesus Christ who taught you this, and we are
convinced of it, we will love Him and we will follow Him. We
will worship Him because He is saving the world.

Excuse us if we sound a little hysterical. We *are* hysterical. We
are torn between a great ecstasy and a great fear. We are filled
with unutterable hope; but what we desperately fear is that your
hand will begin to be withdrawn; that we will awaken and find
that we were again deluded. We fear that we will still hear the
voice of the communists saying: "We told you they were frauds;
we are your only hope."

We love our children just like you love yours. We don't want
them to be afraid as we have been afraid, to suffer as we have
suffered, and to be hungry as we have hungered. It is more for
them than for ourselves that we are thinking now. We want our
children to be happy like your children, and healthy like your
children. You understand that. Every human being understands
that.

In the past, our religion told us that we were put here by fate,
that fate had meant us to be in poverty, that we were in a wheel
of destiny and must be submissive, that if we endured it patiently we might have a better incarnation the next time.

We have heard your voices from the West, giving us hope.
Your missionaries say that Jesus came "to set at liberty them that
are bruised." We have heard a little of your Declaration of Independence, saying that all men have a right to "life, liberty,
and the pursuit of happiness." And we have seen you overflowing
with health and vitality. We have believed that you want all
men to be that way, that that is your religion, that that is your
democracy.

And so we have thrown out the doctrine of fate, and we have
dared to believe the doctrine of a better day for ourselves and
our children. We have started on the new road, and we will never
go back. For us, a new day has dawned; and nobody can make
us believe again that we and our children are fated to be hungry
and sick, to be exploited and afraid. We are coming up, and we

are going to accept the hand of any friend who offers to bring us up. We thank you that you have offered that hand, and that you have done so wonderfully these past few years. Thank you!

But with that thanks is a great and horrible fear that you didn't mean it, that you were only frightened into pretending.

Yours, from the depths to the heights,

The Silent Billion

CHAPTER 2

WE ARE MAKING OUR CHOICE

TWO FACTS NOW STAND OUT SO CLEARLY THAT NO STUDENT OF world affairs can fail to see them:

1. The three-fifths of the people of the world who are illiterate, and another fifth who are nearly illiterate, have been changing from sullen despair to grim determination to better their condition, and to come up out of their misery. They are uncertain whether to follow communist promises toward better conditions—they are too ignorant to know whether the promises are true or false—or to follow the free democratic way.
2. The one-fifth of the human race at the top of society, which has always looked upon the depressed four-fifths as a legitimate field for exploitation, is acquiring a new, ever more intense concern for that four-fifths. We who belong to the privileged minority are learning one by one to practice compassion.

This book is about that new compassion. It is the most important theme in the world at the present time. The masses are coming up as inexorably as the tides; and the educated, privileged classes are likely to be destroyed by that oncoming tide if they try to resist it. *We are running a race between compassion and suicide.*

Most of us people on top are still suffering from two illusions. The first illusion is that communism is the greatest problem which we confront. It is *not* the basic disease. The greatest illness on earth today is the hunger and distress which gave birth to communism! There never was any communism in Russia or China or Guatemala or India or South Africa or France or Italy without something rotten for communism to feed on—hunger, hopeless debt, sick bodies and sick minds, and the sullen resentment caused by oppression. *Hunger* is the world's chief problem—not alone hunger of the stomach, but hunger for all those things which relieve poverty of body, mind, and soul.

The second illusion which most of us have is that our hope lies in armies and atom bombs and missiles. That illusion could be fatal! The multitudes are not going to be cowed by fear. Our million soldiers stationed abroad do not make them love us. The more we talk about bombs and missiles, the more these multitudes will hate us.

On the other hand, the more we help them to help themselves, the more they love us. This is the one clear, straight road for us to follow. Thank God, it is the Christian road.

Can we do it? We can. The hungry multitudes *want* to be helped. They are reaching up their hands, imploring us to help them. Thank God, also, in most countries the educated aristocratic fringe in power at the top is frightened enough by the communist threats to welcome our aid when we try to help their hungry multitudes. Where they are indifferent, as King Farouk was, they are going to be swept out of power as he was.

It is fantastically cheap, as compared to our military efforts to protect the world. In fact, in the long run it will bring world prosperity. It will be the greatest bargain from the viewpoint of ultimate gain that Americans or the world ever made!

In proving this, I have an easy task. The evidence is tremendous! Man can now produce more than enough to feed the world. We have enough brains and machines. *All we lack is the heart to do it.*

While this is easy to prove, it is not easy to put into practice. When we try to induce men to practice it, we run straight against this stubborn fact: our whole business economy is based on selfishness. We are living in a very selfish world where it is customary for men to take advantage of the needs and misfortunes of other men to make money. Even though the world is on the very brink of world suicide, they keep asking how selfish they dare to be, and still get by. Our present ethical standard is what President Eisenhower calls "enlightened self-interest."

This is all that makes the problem complicated. We will not face the simple truth, which is that there is *no* other way to save our world than to pay the price necessary to lift it out of its desperate misery. We do not practice nor even understand the religion most of us profess.

The most tragic fact in the world is that so many people who have professed the Christian religion and joined Christian churches refuse to accept Christ's Way. They hear it, and agree that it is fine. But they do not practice it.

Christianity has become for them a life insurance policy, lulling them into a sense of false security. When magnificent temples and cathedrals are full of such people, they are like the dead shells on the seashore—echoing, with the life gone. There are dead churches in Lebanon and Jerusalem, in Germany, in Travancore, dead churches in North Africa and America and Europe which have lost the radiant compassion of that Spirit-filled, crusading, miraculous company at Pentecost. After the first Pentecost, they went forth to save the world! That passion to save the world almost died. This is proven by our foreign missions giving. The average giving of church members for our entire foreign missions program is only half a cent a day! And our church gifts for agricultural experts to lift the world out of *hunger?* They average three cents a year per member!

A church as dead as that to the most acute world need is not the Christian answer to the furious, pitiless passion of communism.

The threat of communism has been very good for the Christian church, because it has shaken her self-righteousness and made her see her sin.

Communism means slavery to the masses. It destroys all liberty of the individual. It has murdered more than sixty millions. Nevertheless, communism is a judgment upon us free people. The communists have done what they ought not to have done, but *we have left undone what we ought to have done.* China would never have gone communist if we had sent agriculturists to help her improve her farming, and so to help herself out of hunger and poverty. We lost one-fourth of the human race because we did nothing about their hunger.

Unless we rise to a new level of compassion and help the rest of the world up the free way, they will try communism. There is no evading that issue.

For years we nursed the belief that communism in Russia and China would ultimately destroy itself. I had hoped it might, and so did you. But the best information coming from those two countries shows that they are gradually improving their economic condition. They may yet be overthrown from within, but there are few signs of it now. We had better face the possibility that China may improve more rapidly than the rest of Asia. Everybody in China is compelled to get up at five in the morning every day and work hard, following exactly the program laid out by the state—obey or die. Six hundred million people are working under one plan. To the ancient type of absolutism which ruled the world for thousands of years and produced the wonders of Egypt and Babylon and Rome, there has now been added a new thing—modern science. China is spending relatively little on military preparation. She is toiling for economic progress. It is quite possible that she may forge ahead of the rest of Asia, and of Russia, and even of Europe before this century ends. *Look* magazine printed an article saying that "the menace of

China" was that she might prosper so much that all Asia and Africa would follow her.

So if we do not help the world up the free way, the communists may lift it up the slave way. If that happens, it will be impossible for us to remain free. We will have to arm ourselves and regiment ourselves as rigidly as they regiment themselves, losing some of our liberty in an effort to save liberty.

Hitherto we have been isolationists. We used to live in many little worlds separated by oceans and mountains and deserts and wide plains. In those days we could take any attitude we chose toward distant people. But in this air age the world has become one world, and that makes our old selfishness no longer possible. Today, when no land is more than a few hours away, we can no longer ignore those multitudes of sick and hungry people.

We cannot remain aloof and stay free. We must take our choice: compassion for the hungry multitudes or catastrophe for ourselves.

Each one of us inside his own soul must decide how swiftly he can change. You are deciding—and I am. I am clinging to the faith that our change will be big enough, and that it will not be too late. Prove it? I can't.

Studdert-Kennedy, in his great poem, "Faith," says it like this:

> How is it proved?
> It isn't proved, you fool! It can't be proved.
> How can you prove a victory before it's won?

We have perhaps five more years, perhaps even ten. We are running a cosmic race with time. The real question is: How many of us Americans and our allies at the top will choose to put "service before self" into action? This is a race for survival.

Fortunately, there is a great deal more spiritual hunger in America than we have had in fifty years, perhaps in all our history. Real religion is on the increase on Capitol Hill.

But best of all, there is a vastly greater interest in meeting human needs the world over. Indeed, the difference is so great at the point of compassion that we have turned a corner in history. If this is true, we are making the greatest ethical advance in the history of the human race.

It *must* be true! We *must* believe it, and make it true! We must spread it with contagious enthusiasm. The only alternative is human slavery or complete annihilation. No educated person will consider this an overstatement. It is realism, and it is facing grim facts.

CHAPTER 3

THE HIGHEST COMPASSION WAS BORN
ON CHRISTMAS DAY

COMPASSION FOR THOSE WHO SUFFER IS SO INSTINCTIVE AND UNI-
versal that only hardened criminals or madmen can wholly crush
their humane instincts. When we see pain we envisage ourselves
suffering, and we feel so wretched that we either try to alleviate
the agony of the sufferer or we flee from it and try to forget.

But there are higher levels of compassion which have been
reached by the world's noblest souls. At least two of the great
religions which arose before Jesus preached this higher compassion.

Buddhism taught it in passages like these:

Even as a mother, as long as she doth live, watches over her child,
her only child, even so should one practice an all-embracing mind
unto all beings . . . a boundless good will for all the world.[1]

Practice kindliness . . . for so all enmity will be abandoned. Practice compassion . . . for so all vexation will be abandoned. Practice
sympathy . . . for so all aversion will be abandoned.[2]

[1] *Some Sayings of the Buddha,* translated by F. L. Woodward (New York:
Oxford Press), p. 65.
[2] *Ibid.,* p. 88.

When all men speak evil of you, thus must you train yourselves
. . . no evil word will we send forth, but compassionate of others'
welfare will we abide, of kindly heart without resentment . . . we
will suffuse the whole world with loving thoughts, far-reaching, wide-
spreading, boundless . . . free from all ill will.[3]

That was Buddhism, and it was beautiful.

When we turn to the Hebrew Scriptures, we find magnificent
passages like this: "Thou shalt open thine hand wide unto thy
brother, to thy poor and to thy needy. . . ." The Proverbs say
that a virtuous woman ". . . reacheth forth her hands to the
needy," and that "a good man is a father to the needy, and causes
the widow's heart to sing for joy."

Isaiah exhorts oppressors to ". . . undo the heavy burdens . . .
let the oppressed go free . . . break every yoke . . . deal thy
bread to the hungry, and . . . bring the poor that are cast out to
thy house. When thou seest the naked . . . cover him . . . draw
out thy soul to the hungry. . . ."

In ancient Israel, if a man gave less than one-tenth of his
means to charity, they said he had an "evil eye." To this day, the
philanthropy of Jews for their own people is unsurpassed.

The noblest statement of the Old Testament about man's duty
to man was uttered by Micah: ". . . what doth the Lord require
of thee, but to do justly, and to love mercy, and to walk humbly
with thy God?" That was the highest ethical level reached before
Jesus.

But when Jesus came, He demanded far more!

Every day of His life, He himself went much further than doing
justly and loving mercy and walking humbly. Every day, *He
was out on the road hunting for people who needed help,* and
helping them wherever He found them. That was the way He
lived, and that is the way He demands that his followers live.
Others thought it was enough for them not to take unfair advantage of needy persons. Jesus went out looking for the needy,
to save them from despair.

[3] *Ibid.*, p. 97.

There is a world of difference between *not harming people,* and actually *seeking out people in order to help them.*

There are two kinds of compassion. One man accidentally meets a beggar and to salve his uneasy conscience he throws the beggar a coin or gives him a meal; then he goes away and forgets the beggar as soon as he can. He has perhaps quieted his conscience, but he has not helped the beggar! He has only postponed the beggar's hunger until tomorrow.

In this book, we are talking about something far different. We are talking about the compassion which seeks out all the beggars to the ends of the earth, and helps them out of their ignorance and poverty and disease—up, up until they are living joyous, useful, abundant lives in this world, and hoping to be members of God's family in the next one.

The noblest characters before Jesus had taught a benign good will toward men, no matter how weak or wicked they might be. But the compassion of Jesus was not just a benign good will toward weakness and evil. He loved men too much to leave them as they were, or to wink at their weakness and sins. He had a passionate yearning for men to be born again, for they were not good enough. He loved people for what He could make out of them, for their possibilities, for the perfect pattern which they had failed to attain. He loved them so much that He wanted them to fulfill their destiny—to become magnificent sons of God!

Compassion that went out seeking the lost was born on Christmas Day!

It is true that we do care for our own children and grandchildren this way. We start to help them the day they are born, and continue to watch them and help them and hope for them until they are full grown, indeed, as long as we live. Anyone who does not feel this way toward his own child we call an unnatural parent. If we are decent, we love our nearest relatives and perhaps our dearest friends at least this much.

But toward unfortunate people outside our family circles we do not feel the same solicitude, nor the same sense of responsibility—not unless we have caught the strange, all-embracing compassion of Jesus.

Jesus Christ felt the same eager desire for *everybody in need* that we feel for our children and for our closest relatives. Every child was His child. All of them were, as He said, "My brother, and sister, and mother." This attitude toward the whole human race was a new phenomenon in history. We may truthfully say that compassion like that of Jesus was born on Christmas Day. One fails to find it in any human being or in any religion before the days of Jesus.

Open the pages of the gospels and you find Jesus spending all His time every day, all day, lifting people out of their misery and sin. Every minute of His waking hours was devoted to healing and helping and feeding and saving, except when He retreated to solitary prayer to renew His strength.

What nobody else did at all for the multitudes before, He did all the time.

His life is perfectly described in the song:

> Jesus, Thou art all compassion,
> Pure, unbounded love Thou art.

The compassion of Jesus was indeed unbounded. Any stranger of any faith or race in need anywhere called forth His compassion and His help. He did not stop with feeling sorry. He did the thing each man needed most. He healed the lepers. He opened the eyes of the blind. He fed the hungry. He never threw a coin to a beggar! He healed him of his disease or blindness, so that he no longer needed to beg. He healed twisted minds and sinsick souls. He always finished His job before He left the person who had been in trouble, so that the healed man could help himself.

Jesus was the first man in all history who devoted His entire life to *permanent* cures. He could not tolerate halfway measures. He completely healed body, mind, and soul. Many others have served mankind nobly since then, but it is easy to trace their inspiration to Jesus.

He declared that God does not want men to be the way they are, in destitution or oppression or despair or sin. "All things are possible," He said, "to him that believeth."

At the opening of His ministry, He stood up in His home synagogue in Nazareth and read the words from Isaiah which wonderfully described His mission:

The Spirit of the Lord is upon me,
because he has anointed me to preach good news to the poor.
He has sent me to proclaim release to the captives
and recovering of sight to the blind,
to set at liberty those who are oppressed,
to proclaim the acceptable year of the Lord. (Luke 4:18, 19, rsv.)

His compassion for the poor, the hungry, the hated, the oppressed, is all through the gospels:

Blessed are you poor, for yours is the kingdom of God.
Blessed are you that hunger now, for you shall be satisfied.
Blessed are you that weep now, for you shall laugh. (Luke 6:20, 21, rsv.)

He practiced what He preached. Every day, He was *doing* something to relieve those in misery. Here is a perfect picture of His whole public life, condensed into one paragraph:

Jesus went about all the cities and villages, teaching in their synagogues and preaching the gospel of the kingdom, and healing every disease and every infirmity. When he saw the crowds, he had compassion for them, because they were harassed and helpless, like sheep without a shepherd. (Matthew 9:35, 36, rsv.)

When they were hungry, this happened:

As he went ashore he saw a great throng; and he had compassion on them, and healed their sick. When it was evening, the disciples came to him and said, "This is a lonely place, and the day is now over; send the crowds away to go into the villages and buy food for themselves." Jesus said, "They need not go away; you give them something to eat."

They said to him, "We have only five loaves here and two fish." And he said, "Bring them here to me." Then he ordered the crowds to sit down on the grass; and taking the five loaves and the two fish he looked up to heaven, and blessed, and broke and gave the loaves to the disciples, and the disciples gave them to the crowds. And they all ate and were satisfied. And they took up twelve baskets full of the broken pieces left over. And those who ate were about five thousand men, besides women and children. (Matthew 14:14–21, RSV.)

When He met blind men, this happened:

. . . two blind men sitting by the roadside, when they heard that Jesus was passing by, cried out, "Have mercy on us, Son of David!" . . . Jesus stopped and called them, saying, "What do you want me to do for you?" They said to him, "Lord, let our eyes be opened." . . . Jesus in pity touched their eyes, and immediately they received their sight and followed him. (Matthew 20:30–34, RSV.)

When He met lepers, this happened:

. . . a leper came to him beseeching him, and kneeling said to him, "If you will, you can make me clean." Moved with pity, he stretched out his hand and touched him, and said to him, "I will; be clean." And immediately the leprosy left him, and he was made clean. (Mark 1:40–42, RSV.)

He had touched a leper! He would contract that terrible disease! Those who saw Him do it were aghast!

Three years of that kind of compassion every day, all day! It was that boundless, powerful lovingkindness that made His disciples more certain every month that their teacher was the Son of God. They had never dreamed that God Himself could have so much compassion. The greatest compliment ever paid to God was that He is as compassionate as Jesus.

Jesus not only lived that kind of compassion, He told everybody else to live it. A lawyer asked Him how to have eternal life. Jesus replied by telling him about a Jew on the lonely road to Jericho, who fell among thieves who stripped him of his clothes and wounded him and left him half-dead:

But a Samaritan [whom the Jews despised and insulted], as he jour-
neyed, came to where he was; and when he saw him, he had compassion, and went to him and bound up his wounds, pouring on oil
and wine; then he set him on his own beast and brought him to an inn,
and took care of him . . . And Jesus said to him [the lawyer], "Go
and do likewise." (Luke 10:33–37, RSV.)

This Samaritan swallowed his hatred and resentment at the
arrogance of the Jews, and took pity on this wounded Jew. Suppose an Arab found a wounded Jew today and took care of him?
He would be doing what Jesus taught, and what He *lived* every
moment of His waking days.

Jesus said:

You have heard that it was said, "You shall love your neighbor and
hate your enemy." But I say to you, Love your enemies and pray for
those who persecute you. (Matthew 5:43, 44, RSV.)

His intense love for the multitudes made them crowd around
Him. They made Him their idol, and tried to make Him their
king. This caused the ruling classes to fear Him! He deliberately
precipitated His death when He rode into Jerusalem on Palm
Sunday, followed by the shouting multitude, went into the temple and overthrew the tables of the moneychangers, chasing out
those who sold pigeons, sheep and cattle.

He said to them:

It is written, "My house shall be called a house of prayer"; but you
make it a den of robbers. (Matthew 21:13, RSV.)

He dared to attack the corrupt practice of the high priests in
the temple, who were trafficking on the piety of the worshipers.
They had a monopoly on the pigeons, sheep, and cattle which
the multitudes bought for their offerings to God, and for these
they charged exorbitant prices. It was an enormously profitable
racket, for a million pilgrims went to Jerusalem during Passover
week every year. The temple officials were made immensely rich
by it.

Jesus threatened the profits and arbitrary authority of the temple racketeers, and within five days they had Him crucified.

When He was mocked and flogged and crucified, He still maintained that divine compassion to the very end. As they were about to drive the nails through His hands, He cried, "Father, forgive them; for they know not what they do."

His enemies, watching Him die, laughed and said, "He saved others; He cannot save Himself." They did not realize they were paying Him the most wonderful compliment that ever can be paid any man: He had sacrificed Himself to save others. That was the supreme test of compassion.

Jesus has made Christmas Day the most wonderful day of the year. The Christian church took an old Anglo-Saxon day of merrymaking and transformed it into the divinely beautiful day it now is. A humble maiden in a stable, with a baby in her arms and shepherds for visitors, has become the symbol of hope for every poor person.

When compassion for the common man was born on Christmas Day, with it was born new hope among the multitudes. They feel a great, ever-rising determination to lift themselves and their children out of hunger and disease and misery, up to a higher level. Jesus started a fire upon the earth, and it is burning hot today. The fire of a new hope is in the hearts of the hungry multitudes.

George Matheson said: "In the culture of the past, Thou, Christ, art the only modern. No one else felt the need and sympathy of man for man . . . Thou hast broken the barriers of caste! Thou hast reached the last motive for charity, which is the right of the hungry to bread. Thou hast outrun our philanthropy. Thou hast anticipated our benevolence. Thou hast modeled our infirmaries and our orphanages. Thou hast sketched our asylums. Thou hast devised our houses of refuge. Thou has projected our homes of reform. Thou hast asserted the sacredness of infant life. Thou hast given a hand to the climbing steps of woman. At the end of all our progress we meet Thee."

Until recent decades, nobody dreamed that we *could* lift the world out of misery and want. But now science has made it possible. We *can* change the world from an economy of scarcity to an economy of plenty. Medical science has made it possible to change the human race from wretched victims of disease into healthy, vigorous bodies and minds.

Now that we see *it can be done,* we begin to see that this is what Jesus Christ started to do, and what He wants us to finish. The Kingdom of Heaven is a kingdom of abundance and health of body, mind, and soul—for the *whole* human race, for this life and for the next.

Now we are beginning to realize that the Lord's Prayer is for everybody in the whole world. The "O" which begins that prayer is as big as the earth! It ought to be renamed: "The Lord's World-Prayer."

"Our Father" is everybody's Father—Father of all races and of all lands—"Thy will be done on earth."

"Our daily bread" means enough bread for every last child in both the Eastern and Western hemispheres.

"As we forgive those who trespass against us" means as we forgive *all* nations in the whole wide world.

"Thy Kingdom come . . . on earth" means *all* the earth.

All this God wanted before we asked Him. Then why pray it? We are beginning to see dimly that the Lord's Prayer is not a *request* for God to give us things; it is an enlistment. God has always wanted everything in that prayer to happen. It is we who need to change, not God. This prayer, all of it, actually is a dedication of ourselves to helping His will be done, His Kingdom to come, His people to be fed in every corner of the earth. This is prayer at its highest, for it is not asking God to shrivel down to our small purposes. It is trying to stretch our hearts to the size of His world plans.

CHAPTER 4

SLOW GROWTH OF COMPASSION THROUGH FIFTEEN CENTURIES

FOR THE FIRST FEW MONTHS AFTER JESUS LEFT THEM, HIS FOLLOW-
ers were aglow with the supernatural love which they had seen
in Him.

And all who believed were together and had all things in common;
and they sold their possessions and goods and distributed them to all,
as any had need . . . they partook of food with glad and generous
hearts, praising God and having favor with all the people. . . . (Acts
2:44–47, RSV.)

The apostles performed the same kind of miracles that Jesus
had been performing. Peter and John were going up to the temple at the hour of prayer. A man, lame from birth, asked them for
alms:

Peter directed his gaze at him . . . and said, "Look at us." And he
fixed his attention upon them, expecting to receive something from
them. But Peter said, "I have no silver and gold, but I give you what
I have; in the name of Jesus Christ of Nazareth, walk." And he took

him by the right hand and raised him up; and immediately his feet and ankles were made strong. (Acts 3:4–7, RSV.)

In Chapter 5 of the Book of Acts, we read:

. . . they even carried out the sick into the streets, and laid them on beds and pallets, that as Peter came by at least his shadow might fall on some of them . . . the sick and those afflicted with unclean spirits . . . were all healed. (RSV.)

That was the picture of the *first few glorious months* after Jesus rose.

But the most disappointing fact recorded in the New Testament is the rapidity with which the passionately generous childhood of the church died down into what Wordsworth calls "the light of common day." For 1900 years after Jesus, one finds that the compassion and generosity of Christ and the early Christians has shrunk from a torrent to a trickle.

People often wonder why the age of healing had nearly stopped even before the New Testament was completed. This is the reason: it was because the sacrificial compassion expressed by Jesus soon cooled down into the petty prejudices and selfishness which we see among ourselves in our own day.

"Love so amazing, so divine" survived *only* among remnants of the followers of Jesus. Even before the New Testament record was closed, the mighty torrent of Jesus' compassion had begun to diminish. Peter, James, and John all told the church to remember their impoverished fellow Christians, who were largely from the poor classes. Paul took up a collection for the hungry Christians in Jerusalem. There was no mention of helping the rest of the hungry people in that starving city.

"Love one another" was the frequent admonition of the apostles. By "one another" they meant their fellow Christians. They did not mean the other people who were equally hungry. Contrast this with the miracle of feeding the five thousand! When the disciples said to Jesus, "Send these people away to buy food for themselves," His reply was, "You give them something to eat!"

He fed them *all*. Yet within ten or fifteen years after Jesus left them, the church was feeding *only* Christians. Evidently, the hunger and misery of the rest of the world seemed enormous beyond all hope.

Paul and many others toiled and suffered to convert the Gentiles to Christ. They had a passion for souls. But if Paul had any concern for the physical misery which he saw all about him, he did not reveal it in his letters. That became a prevailing characteristic of the Christian church down through the next nineteen centuries, a passion to save as many souls as possible for the next world, a far smaller effort to better men's condition in this world!

Yet the compassion of Jesus was hidden like yeast in the world, and its results began slowly to appear.

In Kenneth S. Latourette's monumental books, *The Advance of Christianity* and *The Expansion of Christianity,* is seen the slow development of the Christian ideal of compassion in the early church. The most cruel forms of amusement died away. One of the first changes took place in the Coliseum, where gladiatorial combats and the throwing of slaves and prisoners to the lions, or burning them at the stake for the entertainment of the populace, had been the common practice. As the Christian church expanded, these horrible forms of entertainment diminished and finally vanished.

Christian communities have always cared for their own poor widows and orphans. Slowly this concern spread to all members of the Catholic Church—in the Middle Ages in Catholic countries, that meant practically everybody, for everybody was a member of the church. This compassion also included the care of travelers, strangers, and captives. In this period, the distinguishing mark of an ideal Christian was selfless devotion to the poor, the prisoners, and the sick. To relieve the destitute was an important function of bishops, and obligatory for all believers. One way to do penance was to provide for the poor and the stranger, and to try to set the prisoners free.

Charlemagne declared that as king he was responsible to God

for widows and orphans and strangers. Monasteries gave special attention to the unfortunate, and established their own hospitals for the sick. There were lay brothers to care for the patients and to bury the dead. Many monasteries had special hospitals for lepers.

The Knights Templar were organized to protect pilgrims and the sick. The Knights of St. John of Jerusalem had hospitals under their special care. Other orders were formed to pay ransom for Christians who had been captured by the Moslems. The Church extended its protection to the shipwrecked. It was decreed that if anyone robbed shipwrecked people he should die.

During the Middle Ages, many Christians devoted themselves to the rescue of prostitutes, and hundreds of cities had houses for these so-called "sisters of Penitencia."

Chivalry and knighthood also taught the ruling class to conform their ideals to Christian standards, and these included humility, protection of the weak, love of one's neighbor, respect for women, and even magnanimity toward enemies! In 1043, on the Day of Indulgence, Henry III spoke from the pulpit renouncing every sort of vengeance on all who had done him wrong.

The growth of the compassion of Jesus was best revealed in a new attitude toward women. Outside the influence of Jesus, women as a rule have been regarded as playthings, slaves of men, like domestic animals. A missionary was trying to persuade a non-Christian to allow his wife to learn to read. He said, "Think how proud you will be if your own wife is educated." The non-Christian answered: "Then I suppose you will expect my cows to read, too." But where the influence of Jesus Christ has gone, women have received a new status, as they did with Christ Himself.

When the principle was accepted that women were people equal to men, then for the first time romance in marriage became possible, for women could choose those they loved. Romantic love is a flower of the Spirit of Jesus. It was the Christian church that kept alive a tradition of consideration for women which flowered into the chivalry of the Middle Ages.

In India, Christianity fought against the cruel treatment of widows, especially the tragic custom of burying them alive with their dead husbands; in 1799, the missionary William Carey started the battle against this custom and the battle continued until the practice stopped. Almost as terrible was the ostracism of Indian widows. In the nineteenth century every fifth woman in India was a widow. She was forbidden to marry again. Her baby, if she had one, was often killed either before or after birth, and it was not unusual for the woman to be killed with the baby! Hinduism is now as horrified as Christianity at these old inhuman practices.

Hinduism itself has undergone drastic changes, especially through the stupendous influence of Mahatma Gandhi. The compassion taught in the New Testament, practiced by missionaries like C. F. Andrews, was passed on to Gandhi, and from him to Bhave, then to "Servants of India," and other organizations.

The story of the fight of Christianity against footbinding in China has been told in great detail by Dennis in his monumental work on the history of Christianity. For many years the missionaries prayed and toiled over this problem. As late as 1895, there was still doubt whether the Chinese would ever stop footbinding.

The first girl in central China not to have her feet bound was the daughter of Mr. and Mrs. Shie, who were Christians. When their first daughter was born, the father knelt beside the mother's bed. Together they consecrated the little girl to the Lord, and made a vow that her feet should never be bound. This little girl was later named Mary Stone, and in 1896 she graduated from the University of Michigan Medical School. She and many others formed an anti-footbinding association which helped in the final overthrow of this custom. Today there is no footbinding in China. The compassion of Jesus has set the women of China free.

Between 1500 and 1800 the narrow stream of compassion grows wider. This is the period when Martin Luther said that although "a Christian man is perfectly free, lord of all and subject to none," yet "a Christian man is a perfectly dutiful servant of all, subject to all." That "all" was a very comprehensive word. It included even those outside the church.

The Dominican Friars spoke out boldly against the cruelty of the Spanish soldiers in the New World. Bartolomé de Las Casas, who went with the early conquerors to Cuba, said in his report to the King of Spain: "I saw with my own eyes the cruelties inflicted on those peaceful, gentle people, more unnatural than any recorded of savage barbarians. Their countries were simply teeming with people, but they have been made desolate. The soldiers enslaved the common people and parceled them out by fifties and hundreds, thrusting them into the mines, where they died."

Las Casas, a man whose heart was softened by the love of Christ, was able, in 1546, to secure this statement of policy from Charles I of Spain: "First, all persons, no matter what sect of religion they may profess, must perform their missions without harming other people; second, only one method is appointed by Divine Providence to teach true religion to pagans, and that is to convince the intellect and attract the heart by gentle ways of charity." However, off in distant lands, these conquerors with unlimited power paid small attention to a Spanish manifesto. Las Casas derived some comfort from his belief that if he baptized the victims before they were killed, they would go to heaven. He wrote, "I had the blessed privilege of baptizing five thousand infants. They were all evidently predestined to eternal glory, for a few months later our soldiers had killed them all."

Dr. Juan de Sepulveda wrote a book in Spanish, called *The Just War Against the Indians,* in which he stated that all the murders of the American Indians were justified: first, because of their idolatry and other crimes; second, the rudeness of their minds, which were servile by nature; and third, the subjugation of these people would make it more convenient to preach the faith and persuade them to adopt the gospel.

If this makes you shudder, it is a proof that you belong to the new age of compassion, and not to the sixteenth century.

The treatment of the Indians across the United States was heartless, except where Quaker William Penn applied the Golden Rule. And equally heartless was the exploitation by the white man in all Asia, Africa, and the islands of the Pacific. It was not a characteristic of one race or religion. It was a characteristic of the times.

Gradually, Christians saw that the compassion of Jesus must ultimately abolish war. Several small Christian groups declared that war is unchristian, and refused to kill. These were the Anabaptists, the Mennonites, and most of the Friends or Quakers. In Pennsylvania, the Friends showed what could be accomplished with warlike Indians by treating them as human beings. This struggle against war is still going on. Christianity keeps the undying hope of "peace on earth" when "war shall be no more" alive in men's hearts. The day when at last the Spirit of Jesus will conquer war may be nearer than we realize.

In 1633, Vincent de Paul founded the Daughters of Charity, a society to alleviate suffering. Out of it has come the "nursing profession" for women, and a long time later, the Red Cross.

One of the most remarkable men the Christian church has produced was John Frederick Oberlin, who lived between 1740 and 1826. He helped to build new roads and started a school for "infants." He introduced the idea of scientific agriculture (including improved varieties of seeds), and shielded Jews from persecution. He won the friendship of Protestants and Catholics alike, and transformed his community by his many-sided social program. This remarkable man was one of the first to understand and apply the *social teachings* of Jesus.

John Wesley fought against the exploitation of the poor, and against alcoholism and slavery. He tried to relieve poverty and to help prisoners and championed the cause of labor. His social ideals were too radical for his church, so he had to hold his meetings in the open, just as Jesus did after He was put out of the synagogues. The truth is that the titanic compassion of

Jesus Christ is too big to be contained by us little people in our churches.

John Wesley was but one example of this. William Wilberforce, who procured the abolition of slavery in England was another. William Lloyd Garrison, in his tremendous fight for abolition in America, was another.

Down through the ages, Christians with souls set on fire by Jesus have been inspirers of social welfare movements that later were taken over by church or state. This was especially true in the mission fields. The missionary has been, as Alexander Powell said, "about the most useful person in the world."

From the first century, the compassion of Jesus produced a great change in the attitude toward slaves. One of the first and most beautiful illustrations of this was Paul's letter to Philemon. Philemon had a slave, Onesimus, who had run away, and perhaps had gotten into prison in Rome, where he became the adoring servant of Paul and was converted to Christianity. In his lovely letter to Philemon, Paul says he is sending Onesimus, the slave, back to his master, Philemon, in the hope that Philemon will treat Onesimus as a Christian brother. In the New Testament times, however, slaves were not encouraged to hope for freedom. They were told to submit to their masters as though they were submitting to the Lord Jesus Himself.

In the long period of a thousand years, slavery was gradually made more humane, and in a few regions was abolished. Yet, strange as it seems to us today, before the nineteenth century it occurred to only a relatively small percentage of people that the religion of Jesus Christ meant the total abolition of human slavery. In 1102, the Council of London said that slaves had souls like their masters, and it forbade slave trade. In 1335, the King of Sweden declared that no one born in Sweden should be a slave.

The fight of missionaries against slavery in Africa is one of the most heroic stories of all time. It began with David Livingstone (1813-1873), whose exploration of Africa was to uncover this iniquitous trade, in the expectation that when the light was thrown on it, western civilization would not tolerate it. And he was right. Following him, wave after wave of missionaries entered Africa and fought slavery. In Zanzibar, I have seen the place which was once the slave block, where slaves were brought in from Africa and sold to slave traders who took them to all parts of the world, including America. Today, a large cathedral stands on the place where that slave block once stood. It is a symbol of the fact that slavery was destroyed by Christianity. It never would have been destroyed otherwise. A book called *Ghosts* in the Zanzibar library describes the spirits of the thousands of slaves who died in Zanzibar while waiting to be shipped abroad, and are said to be still haunting that area.

Bishop Ingham, in writing his book, *Sierra Leone After a Hundred Years,* says: "It is impossible not to admire the splendid courage with which those first missionaries entered upon the death grapple, not only with the climate, but with European and African slave dealers." In 1845, Reverend C. F. Frey wrote these words:

I was going to Freetown when I met with a scene of misery that I shall never forget. About four hundred rescued Africans, old and young, men and women, were proceeding toward the Kissi Hospital. They had come from a slave vessel. Some, not being able to walk, were carried. Others supported themselves by sticks, looking (from the starvation they had endured on board) like human skeletons rather than living beings. I have just been informed that within a short time about a hundred of them died. What crime had these poor creatures committed that they should be thus treated? It was the love of money, the root of all evil in those who are called civilized people, which had brought them into this condition. If Christians in Europe could have but one peep into such misery, they would pray harder for the propagation of the Gospel of Peace in Africa.

Missionary A. M. Mackay in Uganda appealed to the rulers, who had been selling human beings as slaves, to respect the rights of humanity and stop selling them like cattle. He developed a strong sentiment against the traffic in slaves, and when the chiefs became Christian they abolished all traffic in human beings. Hundreds of missionaries carried on after Livingstone died, and many of them died as he did, to end slavery. Even up to 1900, eighteen centuries after Jesus died, there was still much slave traffic in Africa.

Adlai Stevenson, returning in 1957 from an African tour, as quoted by the *New York Times,* said this of the missionaries:

Anyone who travels there is constantly reminded of their heroism. Missionaries laid a groundwork in religion, health and education under difficult and dangerous circumstances. What they have done is almost beyond belief. They fought yellow fever, dysentery, parasites. And the gravestones I saw. My God, their gravestones—all through Africa!

CHAPTER 5

﷽

MISSIONS: PRESENT TENSE

THE MISSIONARY MOVEMENT IS THE BEST ILLUSTRATION OF PURE compassion in the past two thousand years. A dozen volumes could not contain even a fair summary of this great story.

Missionaries went forth because they had a burden for saving souls; this impelled them to undergo great hardships and danger, and sometimes almost intolerable privations. They had not been trained for the technical problems which they met on mission fields. But when they arrived and were confronted at their mission posts with widespread privation and suffering, they were compelled to revise their programs in an attempt to do something to alleviate this suffering. When they returned to America, many of them attended technical colleges and took special training in agriculture, village industry, or sanitation.

One of these was Sam Higginbottom, who went to India with a major in philosophy from Princeton University, and a degree in theology. In India, he found they had all the philosophy they needed! What they lacked was food, and this was because the illiterate peasants used primitive agricultural methods. They had twenty-five million cows which their Hindu religion forbade them to kill, but these cows gave little milk, and were not strong work animals. So Sam Higginbottom returned to Cornell University and majored in animal husbandry and agriculture. Then he began a most important program of improving the milk-giving qualities of Indian cattle by crossbreeding the cattle with the best strains from abroad. He also established what is now the best agricultural college in India, at Allahabad.

Three things have driven missionaries to meet such material needs. First, their *compassion* demanded that they do something about them. Second, they found that in most cases *they could not reach people's souls unless they ministered to their bodies,* feeding the hungry and healing the sick. A missionary, facing a crowd of starving people, would be foolish to speak about their souls until he had satisfied their gnawing stomachs. Third, during this past decade, as the countries of Asia and Africa have become independent nations, many of them are refusing to give entrance visas to missionaries unless they have technical skills which the nations need. This is why the mission boards have stepped up their requests for technically trained missionaries ten times in the past ten years.

Here is a partial list of the types of technicians which the Student Volunteer Movement is seeking, to meet the requests of the mission boards:

Agriculture: teachers, extension workers, farm managers.

Administration: managers, treasurers, accountants, secretaries.

Education: teachers in general and scientific fields, from kindergarten to university level; supervisors, deans, principals, administrators, music, religious education, librarians, and nursery leaders.

Literacy Experts: journalists, linguists, graphic arts, printers.

Medical: dentists, doctors, surgeons, nurses, public health, specialists for leprosy and tuberculosis, medical technicians, housekeepers, dietitians, radiologists, pharmacists, occupational therapists.

Industrial: textile workers, builders, engineers, mechanics, industrial relations specialists.

Also: youth directors, hostel directors, housemothers, and recreation specialists.

Through many channels of service like these, foreign missionaries have been carrying on an ever-increasing program of compassion. They have seen the need, and trained themselves to
meet it.

Loy Long, a Congregational missionary in India, says: "I know
no profession which offers a wider scope of opportunity to crea-
tive individuals with vision and ability than Christian Missionary Service." He speaks from experience. In Ahmadnagar, east of
Bombay, he and Mrs. Long founded a sisal plant industry, teaching people to make a variety of salable articles out of the fiber of
the sisal plant—sandals, bags, hats, carpets, hammocks and
cordage. Their colorful, beautifully designed objects are sold all
over India. The government has given scholarships to selected
Indians in different parts of the country to learn this handcraft,
and to take it to other parts of India.

Besides the fiber industry, the Longs have sponsored a medical cooperative, a reading room, mothers' classes, and a boarding
hostel. They learned every one of these skills on the field!

Dr. and Mrs. William Wiser, missionaries of the Presbyterian
Church in the U.S.A., started what they called "India Village Service" at Marehra, a hundred miles east of Delhi. The
Wisers had been missionaries in India for some years before
they undertook their first venture in a village. During one of
their furloughs, Dr. Wiser studied rural sociology and Mrs. Wiser
studied nutrition. Then they began work in the villages near
Marehra, carrying on a program in agriculture, literacy, and
health. They now have two other centers besides that at
Marehra. One is near Lucknow, where the students of the Methodist Isabella Thoburn College do village service under the supervision of a trained Indian woman, and another is the famous center near the Agricultural Institute in Allahabad.

When the American government sent technical experts to
India to help in agriculture and health, these Americans found
their model in the India Village Service which the Wisers had
begun. Dr. and Mrs. Wiser's book, *Behind Mud Walls,* was

required reading for all American technicians who went to India to help the Indian Community Development program.

Dr. Wiser says that his eight Indian colleagues are the key to their work. These educated men and women know how to change the technical vocabulary of specialists into words which villagers can understand. All are experienced teachers, with enough imagination to adapt their theories to village conditions. *They start always with needs the villagers themselves feel,* not by imposing their own ideas on the people. Each of them visited two villages daily, explaining the advantages of scientific agriculture and of sanitation in the language of the people.

These village workers demonstrated what better seeds could do, explaining to the people that if they had better varieties of seeds, they could produce potatoes five or six times larger than the marble-sized ones they had been raising, and the better rice would yield twice as much harvest. They taught children and adults to read.

They find the village people are eager to learn, but if they are skeptical or bewildered, these eight India Village Service workers are ready to talk it over with them. Their village needs a road, but the villagers must be shown why they should give up some of their own land for the road to cross. Their cattle should be inoculated, but they fear that then their cows may not be able to produce as much milk, or the bullocks may not work as hard. The village workers, with never-failing smiles and infinite patience, answer every question. These eight Indian experts are trying to develop village leaders who will soon be able to take over and keep the villagers progressing.

Now Marehra has better wheat and potato crops, sanitary yards, and wells carefully walled up to keep pollution out of the water. Women have learned to sew. Chimneys have been built in the village homes to carry the smoke away. Bullocks have been saved from disease.

"But," says Mrs. Wiser, "the intangibles are even more important than the wells or the chimneys. Children are livelier and better nourished. The facial expressions of men and women have changed; instead of showing indifference or resignation, they register hope."

Now we go to Katpadi in south India, where missionary Jack de Valois runs an agricultural school. Here he fights against famine just as a hospital battles against disease. Katpadi is in the worst famine area of south India. For five years they did not have enough rain, and half the people moved out of the area because everything had dried up. Many starved to death. De Valois had hundreds of marvelous fruit trees which he had planted on his land. During this terrible drought half of them died for lack of water. He had men digging his wells deeper and deeper, but the water level went down as fast as the men could dig. All the fields in that district were parched, and the trees were dying. When I was there in 1953, de Valois had a long food line, giving out "Meals for Millions" to hundreds every day.

With the aid of "World Neighbors," de Valois had well-digging campaigns throughout the Katpadi area. At last the rains came. Then de Valois had campaigns in tree planting to replace the dead trees. He held classes to improve the morale, health, and knowledge of the village people. He organized youth into a fellowship, and this resulted in a marked improvement not only in the youth, but also in the efficiency of the village government. He was one of the factors which brought Madras out of her desperation, and perhaps saved that state from going communist.

We will now go to Pakistan, where a cooperative mission project called "Technical Service Association" is run by F. A. Peter, an engineer missionary from Canada. He has demonstrated ways in which special machinery can be used to dig more wells for irrigation, and thus change desert land into fertile fields. Funds given by Church World Service of the National Council of Churches and several denominational groups enabled him to secure equipment which can dig a well three hundred feet deep in twenty hours. The old way took three to four months!

Peter has been a godsend to the wretched refugees. After the partition from India, Pakistan had nearly 500,000 refugee farmers who had fled from India, and who must make a living. They were desperately eager to work and engineer Peter has led them in digging over thirty wells. He is trying to provide each of the refugee villages with a well and a pump.

Peter's sister has set up centers in which refugee women learn to knit and sew. Many women who had never held a needle or a pair of scissors now have a small income from fine needlework which is sold in India, Canada, and the United States.

Let us go now to Johannesburg, South Africa, for an example of Christian compassion where it is most needed. In the suburbs of Johannesburg is one of the world's worst slums, where 60,000 people are crowded—whole families of five to eight persons crowded into one room. Infant mortality reaches 68 per cent. These Negroes have left their farms and come into Johannesburg to get work as street cleaners, as servants, or as workers in stores and in the mines. Now they are wretched and hopeless. To minister to them came Miss Ruth Cowles, with eighteen finely trained Bantu nurses.

In the schools she introduced "Health Week," which is now an annual affair. They have a health parade in which the marchers are led by the "king and queen of health," a boy and a girl selected from one of their schools. Their slogan is "Where there is dirt there is danger." The local motion-picture company lends its health films for this campaign. Miss Cowles writes, "In 1946, there was an epidemic of smallpox, so we offered free vaccinations, and inoculated 60,000 men, women, and children. In an epidemic of typhoid fever that same year, 6,000 school children were inoculated." Twenty years before it would have been impossible to persuade the people to take this, but now they have confidence in this American woman whose life is the embodiment of compassion. They actually clamor for injections, disdaining all other kinds of medical aid.

Aggrey, the greatest of all African educators, wrote, "Teach a woman and you teach a family. Teach a man and you teach but one." But before missionaries reached Africa and Asia, women had no education there at all.

In China, the Amoy Mission of the Reformed Church in America started schools for girls, but had to pay the parents to enroll their daughters there. In the Arcot Mission in South India, they had to offer a bribe as high as a dowry of ten rupees for every girl who stayed to finish her education before being married. "A woman does not need learning to build a fire," was a common saying. When the first few girls started going to Isabella Thoburn College in Lucknow, a guard with a club had to be posted to protect them from rowdies. But all that is changed now.

The chief elevation of womanhood takes place inside the heart of the woman herself. Both her personality and her habits change when Christ enters. Nobody can question this, for it can be seen everywhere. Even a woman's face changes when she comes under the power of Jesus. The tremendous upward movement in non-Christian lands was inspired by Christ through Christian missions. I think any educated Hindu will freely grant this. Hindu social reform associations were organized in recent years, and take great pride in their efforts to raise women to the same level in society as men. Today you will find magnificent women among the leaders of India, for they have been very quick to respond to their new opportunities.

In Japan too the transformation in the status of women is equally miraculous. Japanese have time after time generously attributed this to Christian influence. Concubinage was a very common practice in Japan until Christianity came and relieved women from that bondage. Perhaps one of the most humane things Christianity has done in Japan, and in many other parts of the world, has been to save women from being married to men they loathe, or to men whom they never saw until the wedding night. Equality is coming into married life. Where in Japan, except among Christians, do you ever find women walking in public side by side with men, or eating at the same table with them?

But it is Moslem and Christian women who present the widest contrast. Conservative Moslems keep women in the house, or if they leave the house, they must hide their faces. Dr. Paul Harrison of Arabia once had to pull the tooth of an Arab woman through a little hole in her veil! Dr. Edward Riggs of the American Board of Commissioners for Foreign Missions (Congregational) reported in 1900 that in Turkey a bride was not allowed to speak above a whisper for a long time after her marriage, and she was the absolute slave of her mother-in-law. That was fifty years ago. What an incredible change we see today! Leading men in the Near East now send their daughters to Christian colleges to get the atmosphere, the freedom, and the intellectual and spiritual opportunities that they do not find elsewhere.

Many educated Moslem and Hindu men refuse to marry illiterate girls, and are seeking educated women of whom they can be proud. To help supply that new demand, a Methodist missionary, Mabel Sheldon, started a "Bride's School" at Buxar, Bihar, India, where in 1946 she began educating prospective brides of educated boys. The boys had become Christians, but the girls to whom they had been betrothed in infancy by their parents were still illiterate Hindu girls, and the boys insisted upon their education. These Christian boys did not want to repudiate the betrothals, but neither did they wish to be so "unequally yoked." So their brides enrolled in the Bride's School, where they studied not only reading and counting, but also cooking, sewing, chicken raising, personal hygiene and midwifery. When the brides learned to read, they followed the precept "Each One Teach One," and taught other women in their husbands' villages.

The transformation which has taken place in these girls is incredible. Miss Sheldon says, "It is fun watching the husbands fall in love with their wives as they see them blossoming into such attractive persons."

The example of the home life of most missionaries has been even more important than other things they have taught while working in non-Christian areas. One Christian missionary home with a Christian wife does more to humanize, elevate and evangelize the village people than twenty bachelor missionaries. A missionary in Japan, Dr. C. A. Clark, says his family had 12,000 visitors in one year! While many came to use the loan library and reading room, the sweet, silent influence of the home was even more educational than the books.

Christian groups in various lands have stressed the importance of the Christian home. China began a "Christian Home Movement" with an annual observance of "Christian Home Week." The National Christian Council of India sponsors a Christian Home Week that is widely observed, with emphasis on worship, religious education, order and recreation in the home. Mission schools are teaching their students how to set up Christian homes when they marry.

Dan West, of the Church of the Brethren, was a relief worker among the hungry victims in Spain during the Spanish Civil War. He saw children eating the grass. "Why not bring cows into Spain," he wondered, "to eat this grass?" The cows would give milk, and the Spanish people could then feed their children. In response to his call, a thousand heifers were offered free by Americans in a single year!

Most of the heifers were sent to Spain, but many others were sent to Spanish refugees who had fled from Spain to France, Italy, and Poland. All these heifers were due to have calves in a few months. This common sense yet romantic form of service was started by the Church of the Brethren, but it is now continued by many other organizations, including Church World Service and Roman Catholic groups. The word "heifer" has become an elastic term, for they have also sent goats, sheep, horses, Brown Swiss bulls, and millions of little chicks!

One project given wide newspaper publicity was called "Operation Peep, Peep." Thirty thousand baby chicks were shipped, through the cooperation of Church World Service, to Cairo, where they were housed temporarily in a former palace of King Farouk! Then they were distributed throughout all Egypt.

Twenty-two hundred goats were sent to Japan by the Southern California Heifer Project. The great Christian leader Kagawa later wrote back, "They have now increased to 10,000, and we expect a 60 per cent increase each year. No words can be found to express the gratitude which the peasants of Japan feel for the gift of these goats."

The Brethren Service Committee is doing many other things "to eliminate the forces that contribute to war, and to relieve human suffering and distress around the world, without regard to race, creed, or nationality."

Being opposed to war, the Brethren have found opportunities for their young conscientious objectors to be of constructive help during wartime. The Brethren have served refugees, exiles, prisoners, orphans, widows, and the aged. When several thousand Japanese were ejected from their homes in California during the Second World War, the Brethren helped in their relocation.

The Friends, like the Brethren, are pacifists but their consciences are plagued also at allowing other people to fight for them, unless they can find a peaceful way to do their part in time of war. In 1917, during World War I, they organized the American Friends Service Committee, which has worked in time of war and pestilence, both for friend and foe, seeking nothing in return, asking only "Where is the need great?" After World War I, teams of American workers under the Friends Service Committee helped French farmers get started again, and other teams aided German prisoners of war in rebuilding Verdun. In Russia, the Friends aided the refugees who had fled before the advancing German army, relieving famine and combatting outbreaks of typhus and malaria.

The Friends Service Committee has earned the confidence of the American government, and of many other governments. After World War I, it was asked to administer a child-feeding program in Germany, where half the children from six to twelve had tuberculosis, and 90 per cent had rickets. Most of the cost of this huge program in Germany was met by Americans of German descent.

In 1940, at the outbreak of the Second World War, when Holland, Belgium, and Luxembourg were invaded by Hitler's armies, a Friends' unit cared for as many as three thousand people each night, as they fled southward. As soon as the Second World War ended, the Friends started neighborhood centers in five German cities, and another in Austria. They paved the way for the German-American cooperative enterprises which worked wonders to save Germany from the after-horrors of defeat. There were ten million destitute people in Germany and Austria. The Friends gave endless hours and untiring love to counseling and aiding these forlorn people. They also did their best to rescue thousands of wandering refugee youth. Wherever there are refugees, you are likely to find the Friends at work among them.

When, in 1948, the republic of Israel was formed, and a million Arabs fled from that area, the Friends assisted the Red Cross in distributing aid to these refugees.

A booklet called "Faith for an Age of Crisis," published in 1953, describes the amazingly widespread work of compassion of this small Christian group (less than 120,000 members). That year, the Friends were engaged in works of mercy in sixteen countries of Europe and Asia. They sent doctors, nurses, and technicians to rebuild a destroyed Korean hospital, and they distributed supplementary food to many thousands of Korean children and pregnant women.

The Friends were entrusted by the government of India with a large village aid program in the province of Orissa, and another in Madhya Pradesh. They are the only religious organization which the Indian government so honored.

Always the projects of the Friends are small, because they believe in pilot experiments. If their pioneering succeeds, they know that larger bodies will continue them on an adequate scale.

The Friends were the first to start overseas work camps for

young people, the idea since adopted by many other Christian bodies. Young people are sent in groups, not only abroad, but also throughout our own United States, to do every kind of work that will aid people in need.

Since the later years of the seventeenth century, another little sect of pacifists, called Mennonites, have had a remarkable history of compassion. In 1919 they joined the American Relief Administration of Herbert Hoover in getting food and clothing to suffering hordes in Russia. In 1922, they sent tractors and plows to Russia. They directed the plowing of 9,000 acres to furnish rye for the hungry Russians, and straw and chaff for their livestock. When Hitler sent his bombers against England, the Mennonites assisted other church groups in the miraculous evacuation in only one week of three million children from England's large cities. They have helped in famine seasons in India, and during the riots at the time of partition between India and Pakistan. They have given relief in Japan, helped to rebuild dams in Holland, worked among the Waldensians in Italy, and served in Hungary at the appeal of the International Hebrew-Christian Alliance.

The Disciples of Christ observe an annual "Week of Compassion," sending their offerings to that part of the world where need is most critical. There are no denominational strings attached to this fund—it is available for interdenominational uses. Four million dollars has been raised by the Disciples through these Weeks of Compassion. In addition, the Disciples have given $2 million for relief and rehabilitation in Europe, and half a million for Asia. Other denominations also have similar offerings, such as "One Great Hour of Sharing."

One of the purest illustrations of compassion in all the long history of the church is that of the Salvation Army. That organization reaches down to what Rabindranath Tagore calls the "poorest, and the lowliest, and the lost." It goes where few others care to reach. It endures the vileness of filthy drunkards and ragged vagrants. It helps people not because they deserve to be helped but because they are in dire need. In this seeking and saving those at the bottom, there is no more consistently and perfectly Christlike religious organization in the world.

Begun by William Booth in 1865, when he was seeking to save souls on the streets of London, the "Army" has been led far beyond its original interests. Rescue work among women was one of its earlier social tasks, begun under the leadership of Mrs. Florence Booth, wife of the "General's" son. By 1918, this phase of the work had achieved such popularity in British circles that a government subsidy was granted the Army to enlarge and continue it. While money and personnel requirements constantly strain the capacities of the Salvation Army, they march on, often with their famous brass bands drawing throngs of idle onlookers. And some of those onlookers are drawn into the stream of compassionate service.

When World War I broke, the Army's United States commander, Evangeline Booth, made her entire staff and resources available for the armed forces—all the way up to the front-line trenches. Their work was so realistic and helpful that she received the Distinguished Service Medal for it.

Again, in the Second World War, the Army's rescue teams from European countries forgot themselves in the call to serve. Wherever they were allowed to enter—Norway, Finland, Belgium, Holland, Germany, France, Italy—their compassionate devotion brought far more than "hot coffee and doughnuts": hope to the despairing, help for the lost, love to the hated, searching parties for missing soldiers, clinics for the ill, shelter for the victims of war.

Emergencies such as the disastrous tornadoes in southern and southwestern United States in 1955 found the Salvation Army quickly on the job with supplies, personnel, and equipment.

The work of the Salvation Army has spread into 85 countries and colonies. In its service in 1957 were 26,765 officers and cadets, plus hundreds of thousands of volunteer lay members. Its 112 hospitals and clinics and dispensaries, its 143 children's homes, its 821 day schools for poor children, its 191 residences

for homeless groups, its 88 maternity homes, its 197 shelters and
work shops for men and its 64 employment bureaus, help
countless people all over this awakening planet. The Army
has touched America's heart, and the heart of the whole free
world!

CHAPTER 6

MISSIONS: MEDICAL

NEITHER COMPASSION ALONE NOR SKILL ALONE IS ENOUGH TO SAVE the world. This is particularly true in the realm of medicine. Jesus released the compassion, but He did not bequeath to us the secrets of His miracle-working powers; or if He did, we are too stupid or faithless to understand and follow them. I suspect that the chief quality we lack is sufficient compassion.

In the days of alchemy, the witches and alchemists hid their secrets as feverishly as the military workers hide their atomic secrets today. The alchemists wanted to hold a monopoly of knowledge about medicines and about transmuting baser metals into gold, and to keep this dangerous knowledge from their competitors and especially from enemies. They wanted their enemies to die!

But medical science has come a long way beyond that spirit of fear and selfishness, especially in the last fifty years. The Oath of Hippocrates, which all physicians take upon completion of their training, says:

You do solemnly swear, each man by whatever he holds most sacred, that you will be loyal to the profession of medicine and just and generous to its members; that you will lead your lives and practice your art in uprightness and honor; that into whatsoever house you shall enter, it shall be *for the good of the sick to the utmost of your power,* you holding yourself far aloof from wrong, from corruption, from the tempting of others to vice; that *you will exercise your art solely for the cure of your patients* and will give no drug, perform no operation, for a criminal purpose, even if solicited, far less suggest it; that whatsoever you shall see or hear of the lives of men which is not fitting to be spoken, you will keep inviolably secret. These things you do swear. Let each man bow the head in sign of acquiescence. And now, if you will be true to this, your oath, may prosperity and good repute be ever yours; the opposite, if you shall prove yourselves forsworn.

Our present progress in medicine springs from our sharing of knowledge. This fact needs to be driven home to the public conscience, for all our progress in the future will depend upon our helping one another, as Jesus taught us to do.

See what has resulted from this sharing of knowledge! We have a cure or preventive for all but a few of the worst diseases, and we seem to be on the road to conquering almost all disease. When we achieve a marriage of science and Christlike compassion, we shall sweep on to a splendid world of abundance and health.

In all missionary social service, medicine and nursing have always stood highest, for two reasons. First, Christ was the Great Physician, and all Christians therefore agreed that medicine was an appropriate service for missions. Second, the need for medicine in mission fields was appalling.

In the eighteenth century, a tremendous revival broke out among the Moravians in Germany, and in the Danish churches, and this was followed by a vast "atomic explosion" of missionaries around the world, just as had occurred after the first Pentecost in Jerusalem. The Moravian and Danish missionaries tried to alleviate suffering, but in those days there was little that doctors with their meager knowledge could do. They had no anesthetic to kill pain, no antiseptic to kill germs, and no real cure for any disease. All the missionaries could do was to express sorrow and perhaps administer an opiate to relieve the pain.

The tremendous progress of medical science in the nineteenth century, and the even greater strides in the twentieth century, have made possible a vast new outlet for compassionate service. Missionary doctors were the first to carry the miraculous disinfectants and anesthetics and antiseptics into Asia and Africa.

Dr. Post, a medical missionary of Beirut, says: "There is one language that all can understand, and which carries a message that every man cares sooner or later to hear. From the moment the medical missionary sets foot on his chosen field, he is the master of this universal language, this unspoken tongue of the heart. The Arab lifts for him the curtain of his goat's-hair tent and bids him enter; the Mandarin calls him to his palace; and the peasant begs him to come to his lowly cabin. If you preach the gospel to him, a man may regard you as a hireling, but if you heal his bodily ailments in the name of Christ, you are sure that he will love you and bless you, and that all you have said will have a meaning and a power not conveyed by other lips."

This is why the medical missionary has a very special entrée. It is no accident that Dr. Paul Harrison, a medical missionary all his life in Arabia, was the most influential foreigner in that country. He was the physician to the king and the royal family. He and his colleagues have effected a miraculous change of attitude in a country where no other kind of missionary was allowed. The recent visit of King Ibn Saud to America reminds us that the friendship of Arab Moslems toward Christians began with Dr. Paul Harrison.

Dr. Harrison was preceded by young Dr. Samuel Zwemer, whose sole equipment was a medicine chest and a pair of dental forceps. Dr. Zwemer opened six Christian medical stations in Arabia. The Reformed Church in America, which Zwemer represented, said, "It soon became evident that medical work was to be the great door-opener, disarming suspicion and dispelling enmity. Doctors and hospitals soon followed."

Cornelia Dalenberg, a nurse in Bahrein, Arabia, gives us a good picture of one of their problems: "There were almost no well-trained Arabic nurses. Attempts were made to start a school of nursing, but it was almost impossible to get Moslem girls to come for training. Nursing was considered to be servants' work, which no respectable girl would do. For a girl to take care of a male was unthinkable. The place of a young girl was to get married and live behind the four walls with no windows, or if she did venture forth, she must wear a veil . . . We see many children half-dead from malnutrition, many children and adults blind from neglected trachoma, much tuberculosis and malaria, and many anemic mothers bearing more and more children, when they do not have strength enough to care for those they have."

In 1894, Dr. Edith Brown founded Ludhiana Christian Medical College and Memorial Hospital, in north India. She started with four pupils. This was the first medical school for women, not only in India, but in the entire East. It was pioneer work, and like all pioneer work, it was hard going. Dr. Brown, in a campaign to cope with ignorance and superstition regarding childbirth, opened a midwifery class. Only one woman ventured to come, and she had to be paid a fee to attend! Soon others came and were paid, until the midwives realized how much they could learn.

Dr. Brown offered the trained midwives a special bonus if they called her in a critical case which they could not handle by themselves. On one occasion she found a patient lying on a pallet in a little thatched hut, with a cow lying down on the other half of the floor. There was no time to persuade the cow to move, so Dr. Brown sat on the cow's flank while she used her instruments and delivered the baby safely. Over eighteen hundred midwives have since been trained in Ludhiana, as well as six hundred doctors, four hundred nurses, and three hundred dispensers or pharmaceutical assistants.

Vellore Medical Center in southern India, eighty miles west of Madras, is a magnificent illustration of Christian compassion. The Vellore hospital was founded in 1902 by Dr. Ida S. Scudder of the famous missionary Scudder family. This family altogether has given almost a thousand years of medical service in

India. Dr. Scudder's father was a doctor. She was drawn into the study of medicine by the death of three young girls near her own home in south India. They all died in childbirth in a single night, because there was no woman doctor to attend them, and because their religious customs forbade their being attended by a man doctor. When she returned from medical study in the United States, she opened a dispensary in her own bungalow. There was one bed in the room for an inpatient, and a window through which she would hand out medicines to clinic patients outside. This expanded into a hospital and a nurses' training school.

In 1918 Dr. Scudder opened a medical school with seventeen pupils. The Vellore Medical College has become one of the world's greatest. Over a thousand graduates have gone forth from Vellore to serve sick people throughout India and southern Asia.

These are urgently needed. India has only one nurse for every 48,000 Indian people. The United States has one for every five hundred Americans. Life-expectancy in India is twenty-six years. In the United States it is about seventy.

The Vellore Medical Center was originally started by the Reformed Church in America, but today twenty-one denominations and forty mission boards from North America, Europe and Australia participate in its support.

One of the most dramatic contributions of Vellore Medical Center is being made by Dr. Paul W. Brand, in his rehabilitation of lepers. Leprosy can now be cured, but that does not restore the awful mutilations left by the disease. In 1946, when Dr. Brand first saw the leprosarium, and the patients lined up in front of him exhibiting their hands, he felt an unbearable desire to restore them. He wrote, "I was terribly shaken at the hundreds of patients who held out to me, as if in petition, the remains of what were once hands. I love well-formed skillful hands, and I like to reconstruct damaged hands; but these hands with fingers clenched into their palms seemed to appeal to something new in me, more than anything else about their disease. God put into my heart the feeling that my chief job from then on was to try to bring wholeness to those hands."

Dr. Brand performs his miracles by a series of skillful operations, one after another, just as our army does with maimed soldiers. He first tried his idea on a Hindu man of twenty-four, whose hands were so paralyzed that he could not even raise food to his mouth. After many operations over several months, the young man looked down at his hands, now strong and useful, saying: "I want to dedicate my hands to your God who made this miracle possible."

But another leper whom he restored had an opposite story. He returned with startling bad news: "Since you made my hands all right, you took away my only means of getting a living. Before you cured me I could sit as a beggar under a banyan tree. Now nobody pities me, and I can't get work. I went to the village to look for work, but the shopkeepers and tradesmen knew who I was, and drove me away. I went back to my banyan tree and held out my hands, but nobody threw any alms to me. Dr. Brand, give me back my bad hands!"

So the doctor saw that he must teach these people with rebuilt hands how to make useful articles, and thus to earn their living. Special tools had to be made, and old ones had to be altered so the patients could hold them with their weakened hands. For example, their pliers and scissors had to be fitted with springs. Carpentry, masonry, painting and toy-making are the trades best suited to lepers.

The methods used by Dr. Brand are now spreading to other leper colonies all over the world.

According to tradition, leprosy was cradled in the Nile Valley, and was spread throughout the world by the trade routes. There are at least a million cases in Africa alone. Some governments are now making large grants to mission leper colonies. Other governments are setting up large colonies of their own, but they all solicit missionary management, because nobody except a man with the compassion of Jesus wants such a job at any price.

Deep in the equatorial forests of West Africa, ten leprosy patients walked out of Elat, a Christian mission, one day, cured of the disease which had branded them outcasts. Nineteen hundred years before, when ten sufferers from this ancient malady appealed to Christ for help and were healed "only one returned to give Him thanks." But at Elat in the Cameroun all ten returned to express their joy and gratitude, after confirmation of their cures by a government doctor. Until Dr. H. L. Weber of the Presbyterian Church in the U.S.A. started the first Christian Home in Elat, nothing had been done for lepers in the Cameroun.

Nigeria has one of the highest rates of leprosy on earth. At the world-famous Garkida leper colony, patients from forty-two different African tribes, each with its own dialect and customs, live together in ten villages, with common farming lands, a single government, central schooling, recreation and worship. It is an astonishing sight. They learn new skills and trades such as making shoes, weaving baskets, tending cattle, and growing corn; and this gives them a sense of usefulness and security which is as essential to their cure as any miracle drug.

One of the showplaces of Presbyterian missions is the medical center started by Dr. McKean in 1889 at Chiengmai in the northern part of Siam (Thailand). Feeling that his work in the hospital was not reaching far enough, Dr. McKean extended his services to the villages. His first achievement was to get rid of smallpox which was raging in Siam. After enormous efforts he procured vaccine enough not only for his needs but also for the government. In a few years smallpox was conquered.

Dr. McKean established one of the largest leper colonies in the world. He started out with six little bamboo shacks, which have now grown into a small leper city. It is famous not only for its size, but for the happiness of the patients and the cleanliness and beauty of the cottages—which are much better than they had before they were lepers. Every one of the five hundred patients has become a Christian. Many Buddhists, including officials of the princes, came to visit the asylum, and most of them gave cottages as mementos of their visits.

When World War II broke out, all the missionaries fled from Thailand. At the end of the war, Reverend Paul Eakin and Dr. E. C. Cort were the first missionaries to return. They brought with them five tons of relief materials, including drugs and vitamins. The government admitted all these supplies free of duty, and Christian and non-Christian doctors and nurses volunteered to help in the distribution of medicine. Every patient was given the medicine he needed, without charge.

Malaria was raging everywhere, because Thailand is low and damp; 300,000 persons received free atabrine, the best medicine then known for malaria. This broke the back of the black market, and made drugs against malaria available at reasonable prices.

When Dr. Cort left Thailand, he received from the Thai government the highest recognition ever granted to a foreigner. The government of Thailand asked him to carry a beautiful plaque to the Christian people of New York, in appreciation of America's contribution to Siam.

Gerald Winfield, while a Presbyterian foreign missionary, wrote a book about *China, the Land and the People*. He tells how he tried to control flies in China because they carry dysentery and cholera. But to succeed in this, he found he would have to reform agriculture, because all of the human excreta was being thrown on the soil as fertilizer, and flies bred in this germ-infested soil, carrying germs on their legs to the food people ate. Winfield attacked this problem by persuading the people to use latrines instead of the fields, and to keep the latrines well covered to keep the flies away. For this and other health demonstrations, he used movies, posters and filmstrips, showing the various intestinal worms and how they passed back and forth from parent to child. Large charts demonstrated how to make a latrine, how to kill mosquitoes with DDT and so prevent malaria, and how to save cows from a killing disease called rinderpest. The lecturer read the printed lecture while the audience looked at the pictures.

Ten million square miles of Africa are infested by the tsetse fly. This big fly does not buzz around your head, as flies do in America. It comes at you, straight as an arrow. If it happens to be infected with sleeping sickness, you are doomed to die. At least, you were until 1949. This disease kills millions of people and hundred of millions of animals. In 1949 in London, Dr. Garnet Davey announced that at last the answer had been found, and sleeping sickness could be conquered. A new drug called antrycide had been developed. After four years of hard work and thousands of experiments in infected areas of Africa, the drug was proven to be effective.

A single injection of antrycide will cure cattle, horses, pigs, and camels, giving immunity for about six months. Laboratories are preparing vast quantities of this new drug. Since the tsetse fly breeds in low bushes, all bushes within a few miles of settlements are being cut down. Thus, about half the tillable land of Africa, heretofore devastated by this terrible disease, can now be worked without fear of sleeping sickness.

When medical missionaries began going to Africa, the first thing they had to fight was smallpox, and their biggest battle was to overcome the native fear of vaccination. Today, Africa is so converted to injections that most natives will accept no pills nor liquids—nothing but injections!

Everybody knows about Dr. Albert Schweitzer and his mission hospital in Lambaréné, west central Africa. It is typical of a hundred other mission hospitals, but Dr. Schweitzer has become the most famous of all living mission doctors, and probably of all living missionaries, because he is a great musician and a profound philosopher who sacrificed wealth and comfort to labor in a fiercely hot region for the most needy people he could find. Every true missionary makes a great renunciation. Only those who have fought temptation to be comfortable, and have paid the ultimate price, can understand what Dr. Schweitzer and every missionary has to sacrifice, and what blessings from heaven the true missionary receives in return. This all-out consecration and willingness to sacrifice must be in the heart of every man or woman who hopes to serve underprivileged people.

CHAPTER 7

COMPASSION FOR ILLITERATES

TEACHING ILLITERATES TO READ, AND THEN GIVING THEM THE RIGHT materials to read, is pure compassion, for that starts them on the long, long trail upward. *It helps them to help themselves.* When they have learned to read, and have access to the books and newspapers that will tell them the secrets of health and farming and child care, they can educate themselves from that point onward, just as we do if we read the best books and magazines.

Sharing our surplus food and clothing is often necessary as an emergency measure, but it still leaves people paupers. Helping men up so that they will never again need our surplus is far better, because it is the permanent cure. Illiterates do not want to be paupers. They do not want our charity! They want to come up. And that is what we want them to want. Giving them the know-how, so that they will start on the road upward—this is the way of Jesus. And that long road starts with the ABC's.

Eighty to 90 per cent of the people of Asia and Africa, and 50 per cent of the people of Latin America are still illiterate. There are not enough teachers or schools or dollars there to teach all these people. Many educated people of the ruling classes have been convinced that they could get more work with less pay out of illiterates. They have feared that education would give people "big ideas" and cause them to demand higher wages. I was told this with complete frankness by gold mine officials in Africa. I have often been told, "We must not go too fast with this! It is dangerous."

Then there were many at the beginning of this century who thought adult literacy was impossible. It was widely supposed that adults were too old to learn to read. It was assumed that their memories had lost their keen edge, and that their brains had begun to ossify. But Professor Edward Thorndike, in his book *Adult Learning*, showed that adults can learn more rapidly than children, *if* they are supplied the right textbooks.

Missionaries have strong reasons for making people literate. First, they want people to read the Bible and the hymnals and prayer books. Second, they find that by teaching people to read they win many friends. Third, they see that only through literacy can people escape from poverty and disease and misery.

But missionaries are notoriously poor. What they do must as a rule be done "on a shoestring." They have to use poorly trained teachers at very low salaries or on a volunteer basis. This forces them to prepare textbooks which are easy for anybody to *teach* as well as to learn.

In Lanao Province in Mindanao we were forced, by the depression of the 1930's, to adopt a new approach to literacy. We were having a flourishing literacy campaign, with four hundred teachers, some paid and all expecting to be paid a little. Then came the great financial crash. We received the news from our Mission Board that we should not spend any money. We called all our teachers and the big chiefs of the province together and told them we were out of money and could not pay the teachers. They looked angry.

But Kakai Dagalangit, the biggest chief in South Lanao, came to our rescue. He said: "This is too important to stop! Everybody who can read must teach somebody else. If he doesn't, I'll kill him!" So everybody taught, and everybody liked it. Nobody died. That day, Kakai Dagalangit started "Each One Teach One" in Lanao.

Every day we experimented with new lessons, trying to make them easier to teach, so that a volunteer with no training at all in teaching could teach somebody else at home, by merely following the line. With this "Each One Teach One" campaign we taught 50,000 illiterates to read.

When, five years later, we told our story in Upper Montclair, New Jersey, a group of businessmen organized the World Literacy Committee. Teams sent out by World Literacy have worked with churches and governments in ninety-three countries, and have helped prepare the "Each One Teach One" type of lessons in more than 266 languages and dialects of North America, South America, Europe, Asia, Africa, and Australia.

Everywhere the illiterates have been eager to read. They know that they are hungry and sick and oppressed because they are ignorant. Often they go hysterical with joy when they see how easily they can learn. They cry and shout and thank God. For them, it is like getting out of hell and catching a vision of heaven.

In the past twenty-five years, our lessons have undergone an evolution, just as the styles of automobiles, or airplanes have changed.

Ninety per cent of the languages of the world have almost perfect phonetic spelling, one letter for a sound, one sound for a letter. You never miss the pronunciation if you know the value of the letters. In all such languages, we plunge into teaching phonetics the first day.

It is difficult for people who know only English to appreciate the value of knowing phonetics, because English is so badly spelled. Each English vowel averages five sounds. Here are a few illustrations of our maddening English spelling:

to		though
no	treated	tough
	created	cough
hear	dreaded	through
bear		plough

English is the worst-spelled language in the world! Even the greatest scholar in Oxford or Harvard cannot pronounce new English words without help.

But in languages where there is only one sound for each vowel, a student can learn to read every word in his language in a few days, so swiftly indeed, that Frank Smalley of England calls it a "terrifying success." He is alarmed because, if we teach the other half of the world to read, we are confronted with the stupendous problem of quickly doubling the quantity of reading matter in the world. And that reading matter may lift, or it may destroy; it may teach law or it may teach crime; it may bring peace or it may bring war; it may spread love or it may spread hate; it may bless, or it may curse. Everything depends on *what* they read!

Literacy thrusts upon us the problem of writing, printing and distributing reading materials which will do men good, and the other difficult problem of protecting them from reading that which will do them harm.

Many people say "Do not teach them at all, unless you can make them good Christians! A bad literate man is more danger-ous than a bad illiterate man." But they are too late with their misgivings. A book written in England, called *Nothing Can Stop It Now,* is right. It is too late to stop; we must provide the right books for them to read.

The multitudes demand literacy not only for their children, but also for themselves, and they demand it *now.* This presents the ruling classes with a dilemma—they actually constitute less than 5 per cent of the population of some lands. If they spent every dollar they have, they could not provide teachers or school buildings for half the children of their countries, if they followed our American educational system. *They must find a far cheaper method than we use, or face disaster.*

"Each One Teach One" turns out to be their only hope. If they can organize the common people to teach one another with-out pay, at home, quick literacy is possible. *There is no other way.* This is why we have been invited to work with sixty-four ministries of education on five continents. We have helped them to prepare "Each One Teach One" lesson books, to organize literacy campaigns, and to train writers for new literates. Sixteen more governments have recently requested our aid. There is no wider-open door for genuine compassion in all the world!

Experience has shown us that, along with graded textbooks, we must train a large group of experts so that they can organize communities into "Each One Teach One" literacy crusades. Many others must also be trained in the highly technical art of writing in simple newspaper style, and in teaching nationals how to write simply and fascinatingly.

"Literacy Village" in Lucknow, India, trained five hundred village workers for the Indian government in 1954. In 1955, eight hundred were trained for that government, while others came from the Gandhi Movement, from the "Servants of India," from UNESCO, from churches and missions, and from private literacy centers.

Trainees in Literacy centers are taught:

1. How to train villagers to teach.
2. How to build a community into an army to conquer "enemy number one"—illiteracy.
3. How to write simply and excitingly.
4. What needs to be written.
5. How to interview experts in agriculture, health, child care, and home life; and to write scientific ideas "down" into simple village language.
6. How to print these easy books.
7. How to get books and newspapers sold and read.

Each trainee writes under the supervision of an expert journalist. If he can find books in English or other languages which contain what he needs, he writes these more simply, in his own language.

In our First Reader for India, every lesson was suggested by a specialist in health or agriculture, was written in very, very simple words, and then submitted to the specialists over and over until it was scientifically accurate. It is written as a story about "Anand the Wise Man," who learns to read and then finds secrets—ninety of them!—in books; and as a result he becomes healthy, wise, happy and famous. As villagers read these stories they say, "If Anand could do that, we can too."

Anand reads to his wife about what vegetables they must grow and eat to be strong; how his pregnant daughter ought to get ready for her baby; how to get rid of itch (which bothers his family, and illiterates all over the world); that flies carry dysentery (which afflicts many in the world); how to make a latrine (unknown in illiterate villages); how to get an iron point on his wooden plow; where to get seeds that will double his crop; how to grow legumes such as alfalfa to improve his land; how to crossbreed to produce bigger and better cows and oxen. And eighty-one more such secrets.

When the government expert in agriculture or health goes to help the villagers who have read "Anand the Wise Man," he does not need to persuade them to follow his ideas. They have already learned these ideas by heart in their reader. The expert asks what he can do to help them, and they reply, "Help us get those plows, those better seeds, that DDT, the bull to improve our cattle, that fertilizer, those white leghorn chickens. . . ." They demand exactly what he wants them to demand, and the expert finds his job easy.

This kind of literacy starts illiterates on the long, long trail up out of destitution toward abundance and happiness. They have discovered that the *true* way out of their wretched poverty is the way of useful knowledge, not violence. *Literacy is compassion* because it helps the helpless to help themselves.

The advance in literacy at the present time can best be understood by taking a swift glance at some of the countries where it is most flourishing:

LATIN AMERICA

> *Mexico:* one of the best campaigns in the world, under UNESCO.
> *Cuba:* a great advance.
> *Haiti:* a vigorous government campaign.

Santo Domingo: energetic government campaign.
Venezuela: efficient and vigorous, under the government.
Ecuador: strong campaign connected with churches.
Brazil: tremendous advance, under government, mission campaigns in the Amazon Valley.
Colombia: campaign under Catholic priest, partly by radio.

EUROPE

Portugal, Spain, Italy, Greece: new, strong, government literacy drives.

AFRICA

Egypt: a strong campaign under Christian missions.
Uganda: rapidly becoming literate under government leadership.
Liberia: splendid literacy drive by missions and government.
Libya: campaign under UNESCO.
Ghana (Gold Coast): wonderful literacy drive under government.
Northern Rhodesia: strong, effective campaign under government.
Nigeria: several strong campaigns.
Congo: many vigorous mission campaigns with government cooperation.
Angola: fine mission literacy drives.
Tanganyika: fine mission drives.
French Camerouns: vigorous missionary campaign.

ASIA

Philippines: vigorous campaign by missions and government.
Turkey: vigorous and effective government drive.
Iran: energetic program of Near East Foundation and government.
Pakistan: strong campaign of Christian missions; government starting.
India: tremendous literacy efforts by government and missions.
Afghanistan: strong government program.
Ceylon: strong literacy drive by government.
Malaya: government and missions under full effort.
Indonesia: splendid progress by government since independence.
Nepal: new but determined effort by government.

Korea: missions program good until Korean war, now reviving.

Viet Nam: strong new campaign.

New Guinea: thriving campaign by missions among former cannibals.

Jordan: missions and UNRWA campaign among the Arab refugees.

UNESCO campaigns in several areas, especially Egypt, Libya and Mexico.

BEHIND THE IRON CURTAIN

Official figures of Russia: 100,000,000 have learned to read.

China: vigorous, compulsory adult literacy. Rigidly censored newspapers, magazines and books, all communist, are employed to mold public opinion.

Meanwhile, English has been forging ahead in nearly every country of the world, even behind the Iron Curtain. It is now the chief *lingua franca* of mankind. Schools throughout the world that teach English as a foreign language are everywhere overcrowded. This is because English is a necessity for important government positions, for professional men, and for all international business.

Tremendous progress has been made in recent years in methods of learning English. Its chaotic spelling makes it difficult to *read,* but fortunately it is not so hard for foreign people to learn to *speak.* So the new approach to learning English is through the ear.

Phonograph records are widely used to teach spoken English. The advantage of these records is that they patiently endure being repeated without ever growing weary, all day and all night, as often as the student desires. A teacher of English, on the other hand, is employed by the hour and soon becomes bored by "stupid" students.

Teaching of illiterates by television began in Memphis, Tennessee, in October, 1956. "Streamlined English," a method which combines story with phonetics, proved to be perfectly adaptable to this type of teaching. The lessons are being kinescoped on 16mm film, so that they can be used *either on television or motion picture equipment.* Two hundred cities of the United States have considered using them.

It is altogether possible that motion pictures, television, and filmstrips may prove to be the most effective mass media for the three-fifths of the world who still cannot read.

CHAPTER 8

NEW COMPASSION FOR THE "COMMON MAN"

THROUGHOUT THE WORLD, OUTSIDE THE STREAM OF CHRIST'S DIRECT influence, it has always been assumed that a small, élite group of princes, aristocrats and wealthy people should have the privileges of life, liberty, and the pursuit of happiness, while nine-tenths or even 95 per cent existed only to serve the élite. The masses should take what little pleasure they could, between their long hours of toil! This condition was accepted without question by the great majority of people.

But there are always some people in every country who catch the social implications of the teachings of Jesus. Sometimes these people miss the spiritual or Godward implications, and devote their thoughts and energies only to the social teachings of Jesus.

Some catch one emphasis from His teachings, some catch another. Some adopt a new attitude toward God, others get a new attitude toward their fellow men. These ought to go together, but very often they do not. Hamilton, Jefferson and Franklin were men who caught this spirit of Jesus in relation to their fellows. The greatness of George Washington is seen in the fact that he had caught Jesus' attitude toward both men and God. This is why he was fit to become the "father of his country."

There evolved in France a school which believed in the rights of *all* men. A group of intellectuals in England, France and Switzerland quoted the Greeks and Romans as the inspiration for their political beliefs, yet they went far beyond the Greeks and Romans; for the Greek and Roman republics made citizens of less than 10 per cent of their people, while the French republic made every Frenchman a citizen. Out of their doctrines broke forth the American Revolution, with the proposition in 1776 that "all men" have a right to "life, liberty and the pursuit of happiness"; and in 1789 came the French Revolution. This movement was the outflowering of Jesus' ideal of the supreme value of the individual, even though it was often promoted by men who called themselves "agnostics." They revolted, not against Christ, but against an excess of ecclesiasticism.

In every century the spirit of Jesus keeps exploding beyond the walls of the church. Forever and forever, Jesus is bigger than His church, which professes Him but never fully understands Him nor measures up to Him. In respect to compassion, He is still "towering o'er the wrecks of time."

Today we are still far, far below the compassion of Jesus. We are just now making fresh discoveries of its total implications, just as they were doing in the eighteenth century. When they discovered the *divine right of every man,* instead of the divine right of kings and princes, they were discovering that the whole human race was invited by God to be "children of the King of Heaven," and therefore members of the "royal family."

Wherever people have fought for democracy, they have used the war cry of the French Revolution. Indonesians in this decade used those words, "Liberty, Equality, and Fraternity," while they were fighting to free themselves from the Dutch. Bolivar used them while he fought for the freedom of South America in the nineteenth century. George Washington said to America, "Share your freedoms with all mankind."

The nineteenth century burst out with new aspects of human compassion which far exceeded those of all previous centuries. Dorothea Dix led a movement for penal reform which is still going on. Henry George, in his *Progress and Poverty*, sought to equalize human privileges. There were many powerful books seeking justice for the underdog—Bellamy's *Looking Backwards*, Harriet Beecher Stowe's *Uncle Tom's Cabin*, Josiah Strong's *Our Country*, Walter Rauschenbusch's *Christianity and the Social Crisis*, and Charles M. Sheldon's *In His Steps*. In France, St. Dimon led a movement for "Christian Socialism."

The American Civil War of 1861–65 resulted in the liberation of our slaves. This was swiftly followed by the three great amendments to the Constitution of the United States. The Thirteenth Amendment prohibited slavery. The Fourteenth Amendment gave every person the right to citizenship. The Fifteenth said that no rights can be taken away from any man "because of race, color, or previous condition of servitude." Abraham Lincoln became immortal as an embodiment of the spirit of compassion.

Another tremendous example of the concern for the unfortunate was the founding of the Red Cross, for wounded soldiers. That story is one of the most dramatic in the history of compassion.

The Red Cross was founded by Henry Dunant, a Swiss banker, in 1859. It happened this way. The Emperor of France was at the time engaged in a war with Austria and Hungary. Dunant went out to find the Emperor on the field of battle. He arrived at the time when the battle of Solferino began. It was one of the bloodiest in history. Men on both sides fought like madmen, and even the horses fought. The wounded were killed by beating them over the heads with stones, and those who were not put out of their misery soon died of gangrene. There were no disinfectants, and there was no anesthesia. Between forty and fifty thousand dead and wounded were left on the battlefield. The field hospitals had been blown up.

Dunant tried to organize some aid as best he could, but he was helpless to cope with such numbers of wounded men. Three days after the battle the fields were still plastered with men groaning and writhing in agony! Dunant put out a booklet on the battle as he had seen it, piling horror upon horror. But he also pictured the incredible courage of the men who were fighting. Magnificent heroism in the midst of horrible suffering!

In response to Dunant's impassioned plea for aid, the nobles of Milan, as well as the common people, opened their homes to the wounded soldiers. All Europe was shocked when it heard of the account of 40,000 men who had died because they did not have adequate medical care. Dunant and four other men formally organized that first society which has become the International Red Cross.

That was not done without opposition. Chief Marshal Billant of the French Army fought against the whole idea of the Red Cross. He believed that captured towns should be burned, their garrisons killed, and the captives slaughtered, as had always been done before in all "civilized" countries. But Dunant and his fellow workers persuaded the government that they would save their own men by having the Red Cross. And so the "Geneva Convention" was ratified by twelve nations in 1864. In 1882, the United States finally signed, in spite of her isolationism.

Dunant received the Nobel Peace Prize in 1901. He spent every cent he had on the Red Cross, and died in a poorhouse in 1910. It is about time to erect a monument in his honor, for he has never yet been given the honor he deserves.

During the American Civil War, Clara Barton organized thousands of nurses to alleviate the suffering of soldiers. Her magnificent efforts were terribly inadequate, because the lack of disinfectants usually meant that a man with a wounded limb would die of gangrene.

The tremendous change in our attitude toward soldiers is seen in the experience of Florence Nightingale (1820–1910).

She came from an upper-class English family. When she proposed to become a nurse to help wounded soldiers, her family was horrified. They said that only drunks and prostitutes became nurses! That was largely true. She went to a convent in France and became a nurse, and then went out to organize the nursing at the scene of the Crimean War, north of the Black Sea. Her wonderful success not only made her the heroine of England, but it also lifted nursing into the high rank as the noblest of woman's professions, where it has been ever since.

During the Franco-Prussian War, the Red Cross was called the "Angel of Compassion." It has been the symbol of compassion ever since. It aided victims of the floods of Ohio and Mississippi in 1884; in the famine in Texas in 1885, in the yellow fever epidemic in Florida in 1888; in the Johnstown flood in 1889; in the Russian famine in 1891, and in the South American hurricane in 1893. These last two were the first efforts of the American Red Cross overseas. The Red Cross was very effective during the Armenian massacre, during the Spanish-American War, and in the Galveston tornado in 1900. In 1902, led by Clara Barton, it came to the rescue of the people of Martinique, who were victims of one of the most dreadful volcanic tragedies of all time.

Whenever there was a catastrophe anywhere, people turned at once to the Red Cross. It lent its mighty aid in the earthquake in San Francisco in 1906, in a famine in Japan, and earthquakes in Italy and Chile. It had 20,000 nurses in the First World War. When, in the midst of that war, the influenza epidemic struck in 1918, and no doctor knew what to do for it, the Red Cross was taxed almost beyond all possible endurance—but it met the test.

When the First World War was over, Red Cross became the central figure in an effort to rehabilitate the wounded soldiers, whether they were suffering from shell shock or from wounds.

In 1923 one of the most disastrous earthquakes in human history took place in Japan. Millions were left homeless. American people subscribed $11 million for food and medicine and medical care. In 1927, there was an immense flood in the Mississippi Valley, and Red Cross provided food, shelter, clothes and medicine for 600,000 homeless families. In 1935 another flood in the Ohio Valley left 259,000 people in need of aid, and the Red Cross recruited 3,624 nurses from all parts of America to meet the emergency. In 1938, a hurricane along the New England coast reached a velocity of 183 miles an hour, and the Red Cross quickly rushed to the rescue.

Then came the Second World War.

Red Cross was everywhere in Europe. When the Japanese struck Pearl Harbor, the Red Cross was ready, and in full operation while the bombs were still dropping.

The nurses not only healed the wounds of the soldiers, but did what many soldiers called even more important, they sustained their morale by writing to their families, and provided them with recreation, music, and clubs. Red Cross had to recruit 3,000 new nurses a month, and eventually had 77,800 certified nurses in action. It collected thirteen million pints of blood for transfusions, nearly all of which was made into dry plasma and serum albumin.

It went into prisoners' camps and ministered to the needs of the prisoners. It sent millions upon millions of garments to refugees and displaced persons in occupied and in liberated lands.

All this was possible because the United States and other countries had provided 7,500,000 volunteers, who gave their time and in many cases risked their lives. These volunteers, more than any other single fact, are the symbol of the new age of compassion!

When the war was over, Red Cross took a vital share in bringing order out of the chaos. Seven hundred thousand children in six European countries received 12.5 million quarts of milk.

Red Cross was in Korea, in Indochina, in Egypt, reaching out hands of mercy to those who had been torn by the horrid fangs of war. Contrast this with less than a hundred years ago, when Henry Dunant witnessed the soldiers dying at the battle of Solferino without a nurse or a doctor to aid them!

The American Society for the Prevention of Cruelty to Animals had been founded in 1866. But there was as yet no society for the prevention of cruelty to children. As Walt Disney said recently, "It's a funny thing. You can kill human beings, and it's all right; but if you harm an animal, you have a horde of screaming people on your neck. Animals are sacred."

In 1874, a little girl named Mary Ellen Terry was being ill-treated by her foster parents. A woman next door, dying of tuberculosis, could not endure the child's screams. She got out of bed and went down the street, begging people to come to Mary Ellen's rescue. Everybody said, "There is no law to prevent her being beaten." She went to the home of Henry Bergh, then President of the Society for the Prevention of Cruelty to Animals, and cried, "Mr. Bergh, you must help this poor little girl; they're beating her to death!" Henry Bergh said, "There is no law to prevent it." The tubercular woman said, "But this little girl is an animal, and there is a law against abusing animals." Bergh said, "She is, isn't she? You're right." He hired a lawyer, and argued in court that Mary Ellen belonged to the animal kingdom. He won his case. The next year (1875) Bergh helped found the world's first Society for the Prevention of Cruelty to Children.

In the teaching of Jesus, we do not find a word about cruelty to animals. But we do find a tremendous compassion for children, and for all human beings who are in need. Yet that compassion for children did not find its way into our law until 1875. Children in all past centuries, outside the influence of Jesus, were sold as slaves and mutilated in the slave market, abandoned and exposed to die of cold and hunger, or were drowned or thrown to crocodiles! The treatment of girl children has been unspeakable. And we had no law against it until 1875.

Even then it was a long while before we grew up enough to demand that cruelties to children must end. I well remember visiting the coal-breakers of Plymouth, Pennsylvania in 1900, and seeing the children sitting on both sides of the chute, black with coal dust, picking the slate out of the coal ten hours a day, instead of going to school. Thank God such brutality to children has nearly ended! It would be hard to find that cruelty to children today in the United States of America, except perhaps among migrant laborers.

The battle against child labor in America is almost won, but in most of the world it has hardly begun.

CHAPTER 9

THE INCREDIBLE TWENTIETH CENTURY

DURING THE TWENTIETH CENTURY MIRACULOUS DISCOVERIES IN
medical and hygienic sciences have enabled men to save hundreds of millions of lives. This is one aspect of the unimaginable
progress in compassion which has taken place in the past fifty
years. Another striking change is our new attitude toward labor.
The nineteenth century social revolution harnessed steam, and
later electricity. It ought also to have improved the condition of
the people who toil. But in England, and also in the United
States, the first result was a terrible increase in suffering and mortality. The nineteenth century capitalism seemed to be headed
for disaster. Karl Marx and his followers predicted that it would
destroy itself, and it would have done so but for one thing Karl
Marx had not foreseen, a new deal for labor.

Dr. Frederick Allen of *Harper's* wrote an exciting book called
The Big Change in which he shows the tremendous transformation which has taken place in the last fifty years. All through the
nineteenth century we were living under the "iron law of wages."
Because there were more laborers than jobs in the labor market,
the hungry man, if he got a job, had to work very hard to keep

himself and his family alive. We were living by the rule "Everybody for himself, and the devil take the hindmost."

In the year of our Lord 1900, women in Boston were getting an average of $5 a week. The average earnings of laboring men were $500 a year. In 1900, the heyday of the big tycoons, fortunes were made by cut-throat competition and by squeezing it out of the poor. Andrew Carnegie's income was more than $10 million a year. The income of his workers was $460 a year! An unskilled laborer got $1.50 a day. In England it was far worse than it was in the United States. Among the mine workers, wages, hours, and sanitation were "a stench in the nostrils of decency." In 1850 whole towns in the mill sections of the New England states worked for three to four dollars a week, and they had a fourteen-hour day! Children like those now in our junior high schools would work from 5 A.M. to 8 P.M. with a half-hour off for breakfast and a half-hour off for dinner—six days a week, in a badly lighted, ill-ventilated factory—no sunshine, no recreation, no education, no health provisions, while the employer raked in high profits.

There was just one safety valve: laborers who could not tolerate the conditions could go West to take up farming if they had enough money and initiative. So there was almost unlimited migration in the United States—the older workers kept going West, and new immigrants came to take their places. There was a constant turnover in the factories and mills. But the West began to fill up, and conditions grew worse.

Allen says that the man who started the new conscience in America was fighting Theodore Roosevelt, with his mighty challenge: "We stand at Armageddon, and we battle for the Lord." He stirred up the conscience of the American people to believe that economics should follow Christian principles. In the past fifty years a whole army of social reformers in America has cleaned out much of the shame of the large cities, replacing horrible slums with better homes.

In the nineteenth century the labor unions were considered

wicked! But a marvelous change has taken place in our attitude toward unions. Today, most employers look upon them as their friends, and work with them for their mutual benefit. The American people now see that democracy cannot be political alone, but must also be economic. The Declaration of Independence began to mean what it said, that *all* men have a right to "life, liberty, and the pursuit of happiness."

The lifting of the economic conditions of the laboring people, raising their income levels, and producing goods not only for the few but for everybody, has refuted Marxism, not by any new arguments, but by the democratizing of industry itself. Capitalism has been turned to democratic ends. Today, the laboring man can afford luxuries which no prince or emperor had in all history. For the ancient emperors had no electricity, no television, no telephone, no movies, no refrigerators, no dacron shirts. The people who make these things are also the people who can afford to use them.

We have discovered that capitalism works when we have enough of the compassion of Jesus in it.

One of the first men who changed the old oppressive conditions was Henry Ford. He first employed efficiency experts to show his men how to get the most out of their efforts. Then he raised their wages to $5 a day, instead of $1.50 or less which was common then. Many of us remember how we felt that Henry Ford had lost his mind, and would surely shipwreck his business. But today laboring men often get better wages than school teachers!

Labor union leaders like Walter Reuther are consulted by government and business, and are now looked upon as strong bulwarks against the threats of communism.

A very important discovery made in relation to labor is that when the poor gain a larger purchasing power, business improves, because the people can consume the products of factory and farm. We have learned in America that when you lift underprivileged people until they are self-respecting and responsible citizens, and have buying power and a higher standard of living, you build up a country of great prosperity. The thing we are just beginning to learn is that if we do the same thing *for the entire world,* and so lift the purchasing power of people in every country, then we shall do two things: first, we shall make them excellent customers for our own products and so aid our own prosperity; and second, we shall make them happy and hopeful and friendly, and thus cut the roots of envy and resentment which threaten to ruin the world.

As America has been thrown reluctantly into responsibilities for the whole world, we are just beginning to see that what applies to our country has got to be made to apply to the rest of mankind. This stupendous advance in our thinking is going on right now, among an ever-increasing multitude of people.

We thought in 1900 that the less wages we gave to other people, the more money we made. But today we are learning to understand that the more money everybody has, the more profits we all make. Businessmen are also gradually becoming aware that concern for other nations returns to bless America. That is a truth which we have begun to learn only in the past twenty years.

Up to the year 1917, the United States was almost unanimously isolationist. When World War I broke out, all America was determined to remain neutral. Woodrow Wilson was elected on his promise that he would keep us out of war. We had faith that if anybody could keep the United States out of war, he could. Wilson himself had written words which sounded like the isolationism in which we Americans believed. We all were isolationists in those days, as every man old enough to remember will admit.

We remained neutral for two and a half years after that war began, and entered it only when Germany began unrestricted sinking of all ships on the high seas. Then Wilson was forced to admit that war was on. He did it in exquisite English that stirred up the righteous wrath of all Americans. But Wilson's great masterpiece was the Fourteen Points which he presented to Congress in January, 1918. Instantly the Allies saw the power of those words, and they scattered leaflets of the Fourteen Points from airplanes all over Germany. Those promises of a better world had more power than the Allied guns had, to undermine the morale of fighting Germany, and so end the war. Five of those fourteen points must be included in a book on compassion:

1. All diplomacy between nations to be open to the public, with no private international understandings of any kind.
2. Equality of trade conditions among all the nations which consent to peace.
3. National armaments will be reduced to the lowest point consistent with domestic safety.
4. Adjustment of all colonial claims so that the interests of the populations shall have equal weight with the claims of ruling governments.
5. A general association of nations must be formed, for the purpose of guaranteeing political independence to great and small states alike. (This was by far the most important point.)

In October, 1918, Germany sued for peace, nine months after the Fourteen Points were scattered over that country. The Germans believed that they would get many of the things they had fought for. But Woodrow Wilson was unable to fulfill his promises. He was forced to compromise on one after another of them in order to save his fourteenth point, which became the League of Nations.

Wilson was too far ahead of his time, and he suffered the martyrdom which had come to many other men before him, to men who saw far ahead. For a few months after the close of the war, Wilson was the most idolized man in all history, for he promised what the people sincerely wanted. But at the very time the multitudes were shouting his praises, he was agonizing at the peace table over his ideals, against three clever and unidealistic associates from Britain, France, and Italy. He lost most of that battle, but at least he was able to have his League of Nations incorporated in the Treaty. He thought, and rightly, that this was the supreme goal for the world. It was the farthest reach toward world cooperation in all the long history of the human race up to that time. The Treaty was finally accepted by our Allies in Europe.

But our own Congress first weakened it with reservations, and then rejected it entirely. This broke Wilson's heart. His final tragic collapse will, in the eyes of history, place him among our martyrs. He had staked everything on a new world order and a new era of perpetual peace. The world seemed to him to be ripe for a new order. Alfred Tennyson's prophecy of a "parliament of man, the federation of the world" had almost come true!

Did Woodrow Wilson fail? If you judge him by the frightening disillusionment of the world after his noble ideals were mocked and defeated, yes. If you asked the people in 1930, during the worst depression we have had in history, they would reply, "yes." If you asked them in 1941 when World War II was upon us, they would have answered, "yes." If you ask in 1958 whether Wilson failed, we might reply that he was the *only man of his time who did not fail.*

And yet Woodrow Wilson should have added to his fourteen points another point. The list he gave was beautiful, but he left out one which I am sure a God like Jesus Christ would want him to include. This was the opportunity for the unfortunate, helpless lower three-fourths of the world to get out of its misery and ignorance, and really live. Wilson, in his inimitable style, said: "There are things more precious than peace." But he did not name these hungry three-fourths who in God's eyes are "more precious than peace." I think God will not give us peace until we emancipate them. Not if God is like Jesus Christ, as Christians maintain He is.

Even if there were no God, which seems to me to be the most absurd of all hypotheses, it would still be true that stable peace is hopeless so long as half the world is hungry and desperately unhappy.

Wilson did say this: "Our civilization cannot survive materially unless it can be redeemed spiritually. It can be saved only by becoming permeated by the Spirit of Christ, and by being made free and happy by the practices which spring out of that Spirit."

The story of the mining engineer, Herbert Hoover, at the time of the First World War, is one of the most dramatic in our age of growing compassion. He was in London when that war began. Two hundred thousand stranded Americans had fled there from Europe. Most of them had no currency, and the American ambassador appealed to Herbert Hoover for help. He responded by cashing American checks personally. Out of the thousands of dollars he advanced, he lost only a hundred and fifty dollars.

Soon after Belgium was invaded, an engineer named Mallard K. Shaylor saw that Belgium would not have any food left in three weeks. He came to London and discussed the problem with Hoover. He told Hoover that Germany refused to feed the Belgians on the score that she did not have enough for her own people, and that the Allies had declined to let any food through the blockade.

Hoover was a trained engineer—accurate, thorough, and a prodigious worker—and he had vision. The magnitude of this Belgian crisis fired his imagination. He hurried back to the United States, turned his business over to friends, and made a personal appeal to the American people. Not naturally eloquent, but aided by the power of the Spirit, he succeeded *in ninety days* in building an organization with thirty-five ships flying the Belgian Relief flag. He ordered ten million bushels of wheat. He got the chief auditing firm in London to take responsibility for the financial soundness of his work, so that there would be no scandal. This firm countersigned all his checks. Ten million starving Belgians received $10 million worth of wheat in those thirty-five ships. Hoover and his friends went into debt to get this food to the hungry. There was never an official agreement with any of the governments involved, but he got the cooperation of both the Allies and Germany. Soon his fleet had grown to seventy ships. The money poured in, and instead of $5 million a month, he was raising at least $25 million! Some of these ships were being bombed, so Hoover went himself and made his protest to the German High Command. They assured him they would take care of it, but he refused to leave until he himself heard the order given over the telephone.

Most of his ships got through. Some did not. The Germans

took part of the food for themselves, or took the Belgians' own food and replaced it with Hoover's food. In spite of the fact that the Germans torpedoed some ships and the British would not let other ships through their blockade, Hoover fed the hungry.

At the beginning, most of the British Cabinet were against helping the Belgians, and Hoover had to go and persuade them, one at a time. Lloyd-George finally agreed to give him a million pounds a month, and then Hoover went to France and persuaded the French government to donate $7 million. Altogether, during the war, the British, French and American governments gave about a billion dollars for relief in Belgium and France. The overhead in carrying out this program came to only $4 million, less than one-half of one per cent of the total! Hoover himself never accepted any salary, and he paid all of his own traveling expenses.

This was the most tremendous single achievement in compassion in the history of the world. Hoover deserves enormous credit, because he had to *fight for the privilege of helping* these starving people, against two powerful enemies, each bent upon moving heaven and earth to defeat the other.

The American government was so impressed that it invited Hoover to head the American Relief Administration from 1918 to 1921. Twenty million people were facing starvation. The fate of the war depended upon food. Hoover went at it single-handed. Although the Allies wanted a part in the administration of relief, Hoover hesitated, considering his experience during the war. Finally an agreement was drawn up with the Allies which satisfied everybody. Relief was administered on the basis of need.

In Central and Eastern Europe, ten million children were hungry. Hoover, the Allied governments, and organizations such as the International Red Cross, the American Friends Service Committee, and many other organizations, fed them with $163 million worth of food.

Hoover's work was a mammoth task of human compassion for the hungry of ravished Europe. It was a high point, up to that time, in the history of human compassion. He helped people to help themselves, not merely alleviating their suffering, but helping them to get back on their own feet. In theory, this food was sold to Europe, but of course in the end it turned out to be a gift, and the $50 million worth of food loaned to Germany by the British and French was never returned. Herbert Hoover had performed a stupendous miracle.

CHAPTER 10

THE ROCKEFELLER FOUNDATION

LATE IN THE NINETEENTH AND EARLY IN THE TWENTIETH CENTU-
ries, a considerable number of men made huge fortunes. Among
these were John D. Rockefeller, Andrew Carnegie, Russell Sage,
John S. Guggenheim, and Julius Rosenwald. All of these became
famous for the contributions they made to the welfare of the
country and the world.

Raymond Fosdick's book called *The Story of the Rockefeller
Foundation,* gives us the secret that John D. Rockefeller
learned to give for worthy causes from his mother. He wrote,
"From the beginning I was trained to work, to save, and to
give." Even when his income was small, he gave regularly, not
only to the Baptist Church, but to several other churches. In
1909, Mr. Rockefeller wrote: "As I study wealthy men, I can see
but one way in which they can secure a real equivalent for money
spent, and that is to cultivate a taste for giving when that money
will produce an effect which will be a lasting gratification." When
Andrew Carnegie wrote an essay called "The Gospel of
Wealth," Mr. Rockefeller wrote to him, "I would that more men
of wealth were doing as you are doing with your money; but be
assured your example will bear fruit, and the time will come

when men of wealth will more generally be willing to use it for the good of others." Mr. Rockefeller, according to Mr. Fosdick, repeatedly said: "A man should make all he can, and give all he can."

Mr. Rockefeller not only took pains to accumulate the money which he had, but he was also extremely conscientious about how he spent it. He abhorred indiscriminate giving, and he had a passion for excellence. Frederick T. Gates, who became a trusted friend of Mr. Rockefeller, had a very great part in developing the most helpful philanthropy of all history. Mr. Gates says of Mr. Rockefeller: "I gradually developed and introduced into all his charities the principles of scientific giving, and he found himself in no long time laying aside retail giving almost wholly, and entering safely and pleasurably into the field of wholesale philanthropy." At first Mr. Rockefeller gave through individual missionaries, but later, upon Mr. Gates' advice, discontinued this practice and gave through the experienced mission boards, considering them experts in the proper uses of the money.

In 1901, in the loft of a building in New York, the Rockefeller Institute for Medical Research was launched, for which Mr. Rockefeller gave $20,000 a year for ten years. Here were gathered some of the finest medical scientists the world has known, among them Simon Flexner and Dr. Hideyo Noguchi. From this modest beginning came one of the world's great centers of medical research. In fact, medicine has been among the chief interests of the Rockefellers, and their contributions in this field have contributed enormously to the health of the world.

One of the early problems which interested the Rockefellers was Negro education in the South. In 1902, Mr. Rockefeller founded the General Education Board, which devoted a large part of its funds to the improvement of education for Negroes, particularly in the southern states. This program undoubtedly stimulated Julius Rosenwald and many others in a like interest in the Negroes. Gradually, by sheer merit, the Negroes are achieving equality of opportunity with the white people of the United States.

In 1909, after studying the idea of establishing a Rockefeller Foundation very carefully for two years, Mr. Rockefeller turned over $50 million worth of stock to his son, John D. Rockefeller, Jr., and to Harold McCormick, his son-in-law, and to Mr. Gates, in trust for the new organization. The purpose of this Rockefeller Foundation was "To promote the well-being and to advance the civilization of the United States and its territories and its possessions and of foreign lands in the acquisition and dissemination of knowledge, in the prevention and relief of suffering, and in the promotion of any and all the elements of human progress."

By the year 1927, Mr. Rockefeller's gifts to this Foundation amounted to $182,851,470.90, and the use of these funds had accomplished many miracles.

In the South, the Rockefeller Sanitary Commission, which later became a part of the Rockefeller Foundation, achieved dramatic success in getting rid of hookworm, under the direction of Dr. Wycliffe Rose. When Dr. Rose began his attack on hookworm, many people regarded it as a myth. But examination showed that more than one-third of the children in the schools of the South were infected by this disease. In some schools the incidence of the disease was much higher.

For example, in one school in Virginia, thirty-eight out of forty children were infected, and forty-five other children were too weak with disease to attend! Three hundred college students were examined, and 42 per cent of them also had hookworm. Three regiments of the state militia were examined and their rates of infection were 36 per cent, 58 per cent, and 32 per cent. Victims of the hookworm tend to become more and more anemic, become weaker, and their growth is stunted. They have protruding shoulder blades, a bloated stomach, and swollen joints. The remedy for hookworm is very simple—capsules of thymol and salts must be taken over a period of about eighteen hours. In order to keep the victims from being reinfected, they must wear shoes and have sanitary latrine facilities.

Dr. Rose first made a very thorough survey to determine the distribution of this disease, and then he started a battle of publicity. Free examination and free treatment of all who applied were given, the support of the schools was enlisted, twenty-five thousand public meetings were held with an attendance of over two million people, and more than three million pieces of literature were distributed.

In five years, the people of the eleven southern states where hookworm was bad, had become convinced they could be cured, and were well on the way toward complete elimination of this disease.

As a result of this early work in public health, the International Health Board of the Rockefeller Foundation was established. Dr. Wycliffe Rose, who had directed the attack on hookworm in the South, became the director to carry out the same type of work in other countries. The attack went into six continents, fifty-two countries, and twenty-nine islands. It was found that hookworm is a disease of hot countries, and that temperature as low as fifty degrees checks the development of the larva. India has an especially high rate of this infection—60 to 80 per cent of its entire population—and wherever Indian laborers migrated to other countries, they carried the infection along with them.

Then Dr. Rose and his associates began to dream of the control of malaria, which disease is probably the greatest handicap to the economic efficiency of the human race today. He also began to dream of attacking tuberculosis and yellow fever. The thinking of Dr. Rose was on a global scale. He said: "Unless public health is conceived in international terms, the strategic opportunity of our generation will be lost." When the Rockefeller health work began, there had been practically nothing done for cholera, typhoid, dysentery, malaria or tuberculosis. Only smallpox had begun to be controlled. The Rockefeller Foundation did not by itself carry out these health measures for all the people, but it did everything in its power to help governmental agencies to set up permanent health programs in the county, state, or country with which it was cooperating. Dr. Rose considered the Foundation's work to be merely "pump priming."

He found, as we always find whenever we undertake new things, that the real bottleneck is the lack of trained men. Then he did the reasonable thing. The Foundation endowed a School of Hygiene and Public Health at Johns Hopkins University in order to prepare such trained men. The Foundation made another gift to Harvard to develop a similar school; and then schools and institutes for training people were started in London, Prague, Copenhagen, Belgrade, Madrid, Rome, Tokyo, Calcutta, Manila, Sao Paulo in Brazil, and in many other places. Twenty-five million dollars were spent in starting these schools to train people in public health work. Fellowships were granted to bring promising students to these institutes for graduate training.

The laboratory in the Rockefeller Institute in New York also engaged in research in better methods of treating disease, and here it was that the vaccine for yellow fever was developed, which now protects millions of people around the world. Here also, studies were made in malaria, and in the understanding of influenza. Great steps have been taken in combating typhus, syphilis and yaws, a disease which resembles syphilis. Yaws causes hideous ulcers on the legs, arms, and bodies of millions of people in underdeveloped countries. It is very easily cured with penicillin.

The procedure of the Rockefeller medical program is twofold: first, laboratory research; and second, the testing of discoveries by field experimentation and demonstration under actual conditions. This interplay between the field and laboratory makes sure that the new knowledge is correct, and that it will be well used.

The war on malaria well illustrates the Rockefeller method of attack. In Arkansas and Mississippi, experiments were made by

Dr. Rose in the control of malaria. He demonstrated in fifty-two towns that cheap anti-mosquito measures can control that disease in the average small town. Then he went abroad to Nicaragua, to Brazil, and then to practically every malarial region in the world. As before, the big problem was a matter of finding skilled personnel or of training people to do the job. Scores of fellowships were given in America and abroad, to train men for work in malaria posts. A study was made of the habits of twenty-five species of anopheles mosquitoes. They experimented with fish to eat the larvae, they experimented with Paris green to destroy the larvae, and with insecticides—until at last DDT was developed, and proved to be far more effective than anything else then in use.

Malaria has almost vanished from the United States, Italy, Sardinia, Cyprus and Greece, and it is being reduced in several countries of Latin America.

Malaria is carried only by the anopheles mosquito. There are several different kinds, but the *anopheles gambiae* is the most dangerous. Until 1930, this particular kind of mosquito had never been seen in the Western Hemisphere. Somehow it got over to the Western Hemisphere from Africa, where it originally had its home. It was the carrier of a virulent type of malaria which is often followed by blackwater fever. Perhaps just one fertilized female may have crossed the ocean, and caused all the misery that followed. Perhaps it came with an airplane which a few hours before had left West Africa.

The next year an outbreak of this terrible kind of malaria occurred in the vicinity of Natal, in Brazil. The gambiae mosquitoes were blown by the wind up the coast for 115 miles. In 1937, bad epidemics occurred two hundred miles north of Natal. In one valley alone there were fifty thousand cases of this killing type of malaria. Ninety per cent of the people were affected, and 10 per cent of them died. Latin America was infested with the mosquito which had caused the death of every single missionary who landed originally in Liberia. It was a far greater threat than war or any other pestilence. This mosquito is very hardy, and 82 per cent of a thousand specimens tested were found to have human blood. It bites indoors, not outdoors, and can travel for a distance of four or five miles.

The Brazilian government and the Rockefeller Foundation together undertook first to contain this mosquito within the twelve thousand square miles it had covered, and then gradually to destroy every last mosquito. Every possible breeding place was treated with Paris green. Fortunately, during eight months, nearly all the water dried up except the water holes in the rivers, and these became merely stagnant pools. The adult mosquitoes were also sought and killed in the houses, with insecticide sprays. Every ship, every wagon, was disinfected to make sure that no mosquitoes were being carried to other areas. During the wet season of 1940, the mosquitoes were contained, and indeed pushed back on all sides, until at last they were in just one valley, called the Jaguaribe Valley. There the attackers surrounded and destroyed every one. The victory was complete. It had cost $2 million. But the Western Hemisphere was once again free from a most terrifying menace.

In 1942, this same *anopheles gambiae* mosquito struck through the Nile Valley in Upper Egypt, and caused an epidemic in which 135,000 people died. The Rockefeller Foundation came to the assistance of the Egyptian Government. The war had to be absolutely victorious; one mosquito missed could mean that the whole battle must start over again.

In Egypt, as in Brazil, Paris green was the principal insecticide. It was applied in the marshy regions, waterholes, and other possible breeding places. Pyrethrum was also used, and a half-ton of DDT was employed in the spray-painting of railroad cars, automobiles, river boats, etc. Within three years, the gambiae had completely disappeared from the infested area. Thus a demonstration was made in two countries of what modern public health practices can accomplish.

Typhus was the next disease attacked. This disease has killed more soldiers than fell in all the world's battlefields, prior to the Second World War. So the laboratories, when the Second World War began, started a series of studies to attempt to produce a vaccine. It was proven that typhus is spread by a louse. The laboratory tried to study the disease in people, but this was very difficult. So they began to study the louse! After many experiments they found a method of blowing DDT powder under one's clothes, and disinfecting a person in two or three minutes. At Naples typhus broke out, so the Foundation undertook the responsibility of delousing the entire population! "Delousing stations" were established all over that city. People came by tens of thousands. They all received DDT, through compressed air guns which shot it up through their trousers and skirts and down their sleeves and into every fold where the eggs might cling. In a single month, 1,300,000 people were treated, and the epidemic completely collapsed.

The International Health Division of the Rockefeller Foundation also has attacked both influenza and common colds. One difficulty is that they cannot experiment on animals, because most animals do not catch cold from the virus which gives us colds. The chimpanzee is the only animal besides man that is susceptible to colds and influenza, and it is difficult to get enough chimpanzees.

In 1917, a tremendous attack was begun on tuberculosis. A great deal has been done against tuberculosis by improving economic conditions and housing, cutting down overcrowding, and using a better choice of food, along with some new medicines.

Conquering yellow fever was the most dramatic success of the Rockefeller medical campaigns. Our generation forgets that yellow fever found its way to New York and Philadelphia as long ago as the year 1668, and that it went along the Atlantic Coast and up the Mississippi Valley. There was an epidemic almost every ten years. The mortality was very high, and people fled in terror or shut themselves up in their homes. Business came to a standstill while the epidemics raged. Yellow fever was called the terror of the Western Hemisphere. People did not know how it was transmitted; but during the Spanish-American War it was found to be carried by mosquitoes, not by contact with other people.

Following the discovery by Major Walter S. Reed that yellow fever is carried by a mosquito, General W. C. Gorgas started an anti-mosquito campaign in Havana, Cuba. Yellow fever disappeared from that city as if by magic. As a result of the controlling of yellow fever, the building of the Panama Canal was made possible. It was yellow fever that had held back construction until that time.

General Gorgas believed that yellow fever could be wiped from the face of the earth in a reasonable length of time, and at a reasonable cost. At his suggestion, the Foundation undertook this task. It created a commission under General Gorgas and began work. This commission found that the *stegomyia* mosquito, which carries yellow fever, breeds around harbors, and is seldom found in rivers or lakes or swamps. Then the long and very difficult struggle began in earnest. It was thought that only the *rhesus* monkey imported from India was susceptible to yellow fever. Three years later it was discovered that white mice, a cheaper and more numerous animal, could also get yellow fever. While experimenting in this great fight, Dr. Hideyo Noguchi of Japan had himself infected with yellow fever and died in Africa. But he did not die in vain, for yellow fever has almost disappeared from the earth.

By contributing a small amount of money, the Rockefeller Foundation stimulated another great medical discovery, that of penicillin. An Oxford University scientist, Dr. Howard Walter Florey, and his colleague, Dr. Ernst Chain, were making a systematic study of substances that would kill bacteria. But they ran out of money for needed equipment and materials for experiments. Dr. Florey was unable to raise the funds in England, and so in 1936 he applied to the Rockefeller Foundation for it. He explained that he had recently engaged a German refugee biochemist to collaborate with him, and needed $1,250 for the purchase of laboratory materials to enable him to go ahead. The Foundation gave him the grant. The outcome of their work was the purification and development of penicillin as one of the most beneficial and powerful germ killers of modern times.

Dr. Howard Walter Florey and Dr. Ernst Chain shared the Nobel Prize for their work with Sir Alexander Fleming, who discovered the mold from which penicillin is extracted.

A partial list of all the diseases the Rockefeller Foundation has fought would also include scarlet and undulant fevers, dengue, infectious jaundice, rabies, and amoebic dysentery. This global attack on disease has added incalculably to the control that human beings now have over epidemics.

Another great adventure in world medicine by the Rockefeller Foundation was the establishment of the China Medical Board. This Board helped to develop medical schools and hospitals, many of them under missionary auspices. The Protestant missions alone were maintaining over three hundred hospitals at that time in China. Scholarships and fellowships were founded to bring good medical missionaries back from China to the United States for further study. American doctors were also sent to Peking Union Medical College in order to train Chinese doctors. That college was also endowed by the Foundation. The difficulty was that very few Chinese had enough education to take the medical training, so the China Medical Board paid for pre-medical education in various schools in China.

This magnificent program continued until the invasion of China by Japanese, who seized the entire plant of the Peking school. It changed hands again when the Communists took over. The Rockefeller Foundation had invested $44,944,665 in China medicine, the largest contribution ever made by the Foundation to a single objective.

The General Education Board and the Rockefeller Foundation, both getting their money from Rockefeller, invested almost $100 million in medical education in the United States, beginning with an improved program at Johns Hopkins University. They also put $8 million into the Meharry Medical School in Nashville to develop a fine professional center for Negroes in medicine, public health, dentistry, and nursing. Every year it became more evident that the main problem in medical education was not buildings, but training more men for teaching and research. They found that without fellowships to aid them, most men were not able to finance the prolonged period of training required to make good teachers of medicine.

Other foundations and persons, like Rosenwald and Harkness, were also engaged in similar programs for improving medicine in America, with the result that, as Fosdick says, "American medicine was brought from the bottom up to the very top." Meanwhile, the Rockefeller Foundation began to make similar efforts in England, France, Belgium, Brazil, Australia, the Philippine Islands, Siam, Singapore, Java, New Zealand, Denmark, Holland, Switzerland, and Sweden. There were seven medical centers which the Foundation helped in Canada. The medical school at the American University of Beirut was given two and a half million dollars. In Bangkok, the Foundation established a first-class medical college, and started a school in the Fiji Islands which serves a great chain of islands in the South Pacific.

Over a period of thirty-five years, the Foundation has awarded *ten thousand fellowships* from approximately seventy-five different countries, representing many races and branches of scholarship. Dr. Wycliffe Rose used to say that he was interested primarily in "backing brains," and this the Foundation has done, to the amount of $28 million. Fourteen of those "brains" have been awarded the Nobel Prize.

The Rockefeller Foundation has achieved spectacular results in agriculture. One of the most dramatic stories in modern times is how corn has been improved in Latin America through the development of hybrid seed. J. George Harrar, a graduate of the University of Minnesota, was sent to Mexico by the Rockefeller Foundation to work with the Mexican government on a search for basic food crops. He and a team of specialists studied the food needs of Mexico and found that their corn was yielding only seven to ten bushels to the acre. Harrar and his associates collected corn of all kinds and began to experiment to find a very high-yielding, disease-resistant variety. They collected fifteen hundred varieties of Mexican corn, of which sixteen had superior traits; and of those sixteen, six seemed to be really outstanding. Those six have formed the basis for the new corn program in Mexico, and also for many other parts of the world. In Mexico and in other countries where these varieties are adapted, corn production has gone up in impressive proportion.

The Foundation has given funds to a half-dozen universities which are trying to discover the structure of protein atoms and molecules. If this is successful, perhaps we will be able to produce proteins synthetically. Work is going on to discover a possible food supply from the oceans. The Foundation has given substantial aid to what is known as the Wood's Hole Oceanographic Institution at Cape Cod, and to the University of California, to make studies of ocean microorganisms, especially the *algae*. There appears to be an infinite supply of food available from the algae in the oceans.

In England, advanced ideas in public health engineering are being financed by the Foundation. In North Carolina, it is supporting a research into the relationship of social life to health. In Egypt and in India, it is studying the viruses for known and unknown diseases. The control of a virus is almost as difficult as the splitting of the atom, and the Rockefeller Foundation is spending great sums in advancing our knowledge of these mysterious bodies, the causes of so many diseases, including our common cold. If the common cold ever disappears from the face of the earth, we shall have to give the Rockefeller Foundation credit for helping, by promoting studies of the virus.

In these days of juvenile delinquency, studies of the Rockefeller Foundation about children are especially interesting. Professor Alberto Marzi of Italy is making studies of the effect of daily stress and long fatigue on children; also, of the most efficient method of avoiding fatigue by planning the school curriculum, distributing study hours and having a variety of rest periods.

At the Harvard Laboratory of Behavior and Social Adjustment these studies continue. What could be more useful in these days, when the biggest problem of mankind is man himself?

CHAPTER 11

PHILANTHROPY

NOWHERE IS THE GROWTH OF COMPASSION IN THIS CENTURY MORE strikingly illustrated than in the number of foundations which have been organized for charitable purposes. Until a very few years ago, American charity began and ended in America. Practically no philanthropic aid went abroad. But since World War I, philanthropy overseas has grown to new dimensions, although America still gets by far the greater share. Since the Second World War, our contributions to relieve need abroad are on a far larger scale; they cover a greater area, and they are more systematic than ever before in the history of our country. They greatly exceed that of any other country, past or present.

Here is indeed a new thing in history, an outflowering of compassion.

During the entire nineteenth century, only seven persons established Foundations in the United States. But the first ten years of the twentieth century saw twelve new Foundations established; and in the second ten years, twenty-two more. Now there are over *seven thousand Foundations*, with total assets of $7 billion! They are giving away more than $300 million a year.

Here are ten of the leading Foundations, showing their assets and past gifts:

Foundations	Net Assets	Total Appropriations or Gifts (approx.)
1. Ford Foundation	$549,397,635	$1,000,000,000
2. Rockefeller Foundation	492,365,671	565,456,661
General Education Board	2,006,652	322,393,355
Rockefeller Brothers Fund	57,274,848	11,240,187
3. Carnegie Corporation	192,446,392	268,450,993
Carnegie Endowment for International Peace	17,329,000	33,000,000
Carnegie Foundation for Advancement of Teaching	12,575,000	1,834,000
Carnegie Institution of Washington	58,978,000	69,427,000
4. Duke Endowment	121,064,000	130,084,000
5. Alfred P. Sloan Foundation	135,000,000	38,083,000
6. Kellogg Foundation	128,670,000	42,794,400
7. Kresge Foundation	87,913,000	43,589,521
8. Commonwealth Fund	81,869,000	91,433,000
9. Hayden Foundation	58,124,000	30,458,000
10. Mayo Foundation	56,060,000	24,836,000

Arnaud Martz, in his fascinating book called *Philanthropy's Role in Civilization,* says that in 1947 there were 147 gifts amounting to more than $10 million each! And three over $50 million each, all in one year.

This happened in spite of the fact that taxation was higher that year than ever before. Martz tries to explain why.

For one thing, it was partly because taxation is so high. People and corporations are exempted from paying taxes on 20 to 30 per cent of their incomes if they give it away. Many persons created Foundations into which they put 20 per cent of their incomes so that they could give it away to help worthy causes.

Another reason which Martz gives is that many incomes have increased with the fantastic rise of American prosperity. They had it to give, and the government would take it in taxes unless they gave it elsewhere. If they created a Foundation, they had the satisfaction of choosing where the money was to go. People get tremendous joy out of being able to help things they believe to be most important.

Then there has been a change of spirit among wealthy people. At the turn of the century, accumulation was the fashion! But as the years went on, men began to be ashamed of hoarding. They saw, especially after they passed sixty, that they would be torn from their wealth when they died, and after they were buried they would have no more to say about it. They saw how fortunes were often wasted by children who were ruined by having too much money. They saw the folly of not using their money for good purposes. Many too were probably worried by the ruthless things Jesus had said about the rich.

They remembered His parable of the man who said, "I will pull down my barns, and build greater; and there will I bestow all . . . my goods. And I will say to my soul, Soul . . . eat, drink, and be merry. But God said unto him Thou fool, this night thy soul shall be required of thee: then whose shall those things be?"

Jesus left but one escape. That was philanthropy. ". . . sell what you possess and give to the poor and you will have treasure in heaven." Over and over, Jesus said, "Lay up for yourselves treasures in heaven," and the only way to do that is to help the needy.

Airplanes and magazines drew communities, then nations, then the world closer together, and so there was a growing sense of responsibility for the well-being of the world. As dangers confronting the world mounted, men's desire to save the world rose to meet those dangers.

For what purposes do the many Foundations give their money? They take their responsibility with tremendous seriousness. Their money is the distillation of lifetimes of thought and effort and struggle, and they want it to count for as much as possible. Most of the men who created Foundations gathered around

them the best advisors they could get, and gave long and profound thought to the question: "What unmet need is most ur-
gent, that we can meet?"

Carnegie believed that peace needed study and assistance, so
he created the International Peace Foundation out of which
came the Hague Tribunal in the Netherlands. He also thought
people ought to read, and so he planted libraries all over the
world. The Rockefellers saw that health was a tremendous need,
and so devoted most of their efforts to making a healthier
world. The Ford Foundation believed that schools and colleges
and basic education were the great unmet need, and have poured
their vast resources into education of every kind.

There are two approaches to the problem of needy people
and areas, one is *humanitarian* and the other is called *aristocratic*.
The humanitarian approach would go directly to the people
and help them, but the aristocratic approach assists capitalists
so that they can give more employment to the poor. The aristocratic opposition to helping the masses directly is that it
spreads aid too thin. The masses, some leaders believe, will
only waste our efforts, produce more babies, and plunge us
all into more trouble. Increase capital in a country, says this
aristocratic theory, and the ensuing prosperity will trickle down
to the lower classes.

The difference between these two points of view can be illustrated in the field of education. The aristocratic approach sup-
ports colleges, but the humanitarian approach would emphasize
mass literacy and elementary schools. The aristocratic view
would let the taxes lie heavily on the masses; while the humanitarian theory would tax the wealthy classes. For example, it
would tax the landlords, and gradually give the land to the
masses. Under the aristocratic plan, industrialization and large
cities develop, and people move to the cities; the humanitarian
plan tries to keep people on the land where they live.

Philanthropy has sometimes adopted one of these views, sometimes the other. Sometimes it helped the leaders, sometimes the
masses. There is truth in both the aristocratic and the humani-

tarian viewpoint. The immense Rockefeller health program has been a striking illustration of the humanitarian Foundation. The Higgins Scientific Trust, on the other hand, illustrates the aristocratic Foundation, for its money all goes to aid science.

When a Foundation is directed by careful, competent men (as most Foundations are) it has many advantages over government, and business, and even over the church, in meeting world needs. It adopts one purpose and focuses all its efforts upon that one objective. It can be down-to-earth and utterly realistic. It does not need to be emotional or dramatic, and it does not need to entertain or convince the fickle public. It is not subject to the vicissitudes of party politics that always plague the United States government. It is not hampered by doctrinal and ritualistic and social differences of opinion that may retard some great religious organizations. It escapes from most of the suspicion of ulterior motives which follows the efforts of our government, because the government always presents the gentle hand of service beneath the iron hand of military might.

A few years ago Syria refused the aid of the United States government. It was so hostile that an American had difficulty in gaining a visa to enter the country. But when the representative of the Ford Foundation met the President of Syria and assured him that there were no strings whatever attached to his offer, he was promptly invited to assist the Syrian government in equipping four operating rooms in a hospital, and to send them an American surgeon for a year.

Another great advantage of a Foundation is that it can do long-term planning, looking twenty years or even fifty years ahead, if it so wishes. How important that is was well demonstrated in 1956 by the efforts of President Eisenhower to persuade Congress to pledge itself to long-term planning for foreign aid.

The late Henry Bennett saw very clearly that this technical assistance is going to be our task for a long time, not to stop as soon as the communist menace is ended. We are now in a very long, tremendous effort to lift all mankind out of poverty and despair, up to a new level where it will be easier to live peaceful, gentle, happy lives. So we need the calm, deliberate, long-time planning and careful, thoughtful, step-by-step progress which a Foundation at its best is perfectly fitted to make.

The trouble with foreign aid through government is that it runs the risk of being reduced or even discontinued every year. Each of our senators and congressmen is elected to represent a certain constituency. Each of them believes that his first duty is to that constituency, and the second duty is to his country. Many congressmen feel no obligation toward the rest of the world, except as it affects America. That may be "enlightened self-interest," but it is not "winning friends or influencing people" to our way of life.

Democracy is the best government in the world *for the people who vote*. But for those who have no right to vote it is as bad as any other government! We never have done justice to our American Indians who could not vote, nor to new immigrants or foreigners. France is a republic, yet her nonvoting colonial peoples have been badly governed because they were the football of political change. If *all* the world were a democracy, and *all* the people could vote, *then* all the world would have the same advantages that we have.

Foundations feel some pressure from public opinion and prejudice, but not nearly to the degree that governments do. If the directors and advisors are intelligent and have a world vision, they do not allow public opinion to defeat their objectives.

Because philanthropy has this advantage over government, it would be better for the world and for America if our government would encourage more Foundations to take over as much of the "Point Four" program abroad as possible. This would be accomplished by raising the tax exemption of donors when they gave for overseas aid. If the government saw the desirability of using the Foundations for overseas service, laws to encourage them to operate abroad could be made with great ease.

Unfortunately, a large majority of our states have put hampering restrictions of one kind or another upon organizations incorporated within their borders. Some states like Delaware,

Nevada, and the District of Columbia are being used more extensively than others for incorporating because they are free from such restrictions. Any movement to set the Foundations free to work abroad on a larger scale would have to deal with these wide restrictions within the states. That might prove to be more difficult than to secure better legislation in the United States Congress.

The strong appeal of the President of the United States in 1956 to business and philanthropy to assume a larger proportion of responsibility abroad must be accompanied by favorable legislation. Otherwise, his sincere appeal will fail to secure a response from the people, or from philanthropies.

To coordinate such overseas philanthropy, a board could be set up resembling the International Development Advisory Board, which had Nelson Rockefeller as its chairman, and did a useful service in outlining the possibilities of Point Four. This board could outline the opportunities and needs for private philanthropy, and could prevent their overlapping.

One of the first things such a coordinated overseas philanthropic program should set up would be a graduate university center to train promising young men and women in the scientific administration of philanthropy. This would mean probing to the bottom of world needs. It would mean studying the probable results of every proposed world change. Whenever we upset a world balance, we get a new problem. For example, improving the health of the world has tremendously increased its population, and has raised the problem of feeding many more people.

Such a center would be more than a school—it would resemble the Pentagon in the fact that it would study the strategy of saving and aiding mankind as strenuously and realistically as the brilliant brains in the Pentagon now study war. We badly need a *Pentagon of World Service and World Friendship!*

Many of the men who wish to use fortunes for useful purposes made their money by "holding their noses to the grindstone" for many years, and thus had little opportunity to study world affairs. Their outlook is likely to be circumscribed, and their interests therefore narrow. Such men usually prefer to give their money for interesting purposes in their own communities. The study of scientific philanthropy would be valued by many such men, as it would help them to see the entire world picture.

The two Foundations which are doing the most wonderful work abroad at the present time are the Rockefeller and the Ford Foundations. The Rockefeller contribution has been so stupendous in the past fifty years, that we have given it a chapter by itself. The Ford Foundation was established in 1951. Its achievements for world betterment in these few brief years are almost beyond belief! There has never been anything nearly approaching it, in such a brief period of time. It has already given away more than a billion dollars!

The purpose, which was announced when it started, was: "Through its development program inside Asia and the Near East countries, to help strengthen peace and international understanding by assisting the countries . . . to help themselves in their growth and progress as free and democratic nations."

It has done all in its power to help education. It started with Asia—especially with India—and the Near East. But it did not end there. In fact, its largest gift was made here in the United States, in December of 1955, when it voted the stupendous sum of $500 million, all on one day, to the schools and hospitals of this country. This was far and away the largest single gift that has ever been made at one time by a private institution. Here are the purposes for which it was given: $210 million went to schools and colleges all over America, to enable them to raise salaries of their teachers (thus it sought to aid the "critical period of American education" at the most critical point—the lack of good teachers); $50 million went to help privately owned medical colleges; $200 million went to help 3,500 privately supported hospitals.

In 1956, $100 million went for medical education; $210 million more went for faculty salaries; $17.5 million went for the Fund for Adult Education; $8 million for educational television; $5 million for development of library resources; $5 million for non-salary teacher benefits. Altogether the Ford Foundation gave more than $400 million during 1956.

Meanwhile, the Foundation was doing a vast service for Asia, Europe, and North Africa, investing especially in the solution of the social and educational problems that held back progress. A proper description of these would require a book by itself. Here are a few samples which deserve a place in this book on compassion. The Foundation conducts studies in: the problem of Chinese intellectuals who fled from Red China; the problem of race relations in Hawaii, and many other places; improving livestock in Assiut, Egypt (these animals are distributed all over Egypt from the Assiut Agricultural College).

Monetary aid is extended to help farm youth of Asia and America to visit each others' countries for a period of months, working with the 4-H Clubs; to the Near East Foundation to push its program in Asia; to The Committee on Friendly Relations Among Foreign Students, especially refugee students; to help village vocational schools in Egypt, Iran, India, Syria, and Pakistan; for a women's college of Home Economics in Pakistan; to train teachers in Indonesia to teach English, which is in great demand since the Dutch are out and Indonesia is free; to help the American University in Cairo to study social conditions in all Arab countries from Morocco to Iraq; for a women's workshop and commercial education in Iraq; to the Friends Service Committee for the Arabs in Jordan north and east of Jerusalem; to a baby-nursing home in Jerusalem; to the American University in Beirut for their Agricultural College; to help the Women's College in Beirut; to help Aleppo College in North Syria; to help the Admiral Bristol Hospital in Turkey to turn out more nurses (there are only six hundred nurses in all Turkey for her twenty million people); to the United Nations to help the refugees from Eastern Europe; to help Literacy in south Italy, through the Friends Service Committee; to the Institute of Race Relations in South Africa; to help improve agricultural development in Indonesia; to help the democratic movement in Japan; to study the U.S.S.R.; for research on the Middle East, on Communist China, and on Soviet publications; to aid agricultural cooperatives in Iran; to stimulate small-scale industries in India and Nepal; to aid village artisans in India; to aid the Rural Education program of Burma (Burma will not accept any help from the United States government because she fears it will involve her in trouble with the communists); to aid study of the possibilities of usable energy from the sun.

The Foundation has established several hundred fellowships for Asian and South Eastern studies to train Americans to understand the problems of Asia; hundreds of other fellowships to foreign students and teachers to study in America; fellowships for African studies in Boston University, Howard University, Haverford College, and University of Natal in South Africa.

The greatest of all the Ford Foundation's programs has been in India. This is as it should be, because India is the largest country outside the Iron Curtain, and the most important country by all odds in Asia. The Ford Foundation there works through the Indian government. It is giving the greater part of its money to assist the India Five-Year Plan. The chief object of this Plan is to uplift the villages. India's Village Development Projects are fifteen in number, one for each state. Each of these projects reaches many hundreds of villages.

Trained Indian workers go into the villages and cooperate with the people to improve their agricultural methods, and to help them with their health and literacy. The Indian government aims to reach all the five hundred thousand villages of India in this manner, within ten years.

The Ford Foundation built forty schools to train the village workers. They are called "multi-purpose village workers" because they must be trained to do anything and everything the villages need to have done. This means they had to learn social education, health, writing for new literates, handicrafts, and village industries as well as straight farming. The faculty and curriculum were all under the supervision of the Indian government.

Great as this gift of Foundations is, it is not nearly great enough abroad to earn the friendship and cooperation of the world. The Kremlin has changed its strategy, and is now out to win the world from us by offering technical services. Shrewd men that they are, the Soviet leaders have discovered that this is the mightiest weapon on earth. They are now trying to convince the world that they, and not we, are the torchbearers of compassion. Meanwhile, American philanthropy abroad has barely begun to scratch the surface. With only 7 per cent of the world's population, we have 40 per cent of all the world's wealth. Millions of people, especially women, surfeited with all that money can buy, are seeking higher satisfaction than the possession of mink coats. So philanthropy may look ahead to almost limitless expansion.

Here, easily and swiftly, we can find the greatest defender of freedom. We shall not only win the heart of the world by a genuine people-to-people crusade of good will, we shall win the hearts of the people behind the Iron Curtain. The Foundations never arouse the fear of neutrals by rattling sabers and threatening reprisals.

Philanthropy which studies what would really be permanently beneficial to mankind, which plans ahead for decades, which has no ulterior motives, no motives except the satisfaction of a good deed wisely done, *philanthropy at its best, is the purest embodiment of the compassion of Jesus that has yet appeared on this earth.*

CHAPTER 12

꧁꧂

THE INSTITUTE OF INTER-AMERICAN AFFAIRS

IF EVERY AMERICAN WERE TO READ THIS CHAPTER, HE WOULD be proud of what his country has accomplished in the Western Hemisphere, and he would be convinced that the same policy would bless and save the Eastern Hemisphere.

During World War II, our government sent farm experts, doctors, and nurses to provide food and medical care for our GI's who were stationed in Central and South American bases. Nelson Rockefeller was made Coordinator of Inter-American Affairs. After the peace came, all of the republics except Argentina and Cuba appealed to Washington to keep the program going for their underprivileged people. So Mr. Rockefeller helped to create the Institute of Inter-American Affairs (IIAA), and handed all the government program over to that new organization. It has been going on ever since. Now it has technicians in twenty Latin-American countries.

The "Institute has succeeded brilliantly," to use the words of John W. Wright, writing in *Colliers* magazine in 1951. Wright said that he had known these republics ten or twenty years before, and so could realize what an astounding change had taken place as the result of this cooperation from the United

States. He said, "People down in South America not only live better, but they think differently also, and they look better in their faces. They laugh and joke as they go about their daily work, for no reason except that they are healthier and happier. For example, in the matter of health: ten years ago, more than one-half the babies of South America died at birth. Now many more of them grow into noisy, rousing youngsters like our own."

Cornfields were formerly planted in bunches. They are now planted in neat rows. Orchards now look like orchards, instead of jungles. Fruits and trees that used to be only for the wealthy are now widely distributed among laboring people. You find tomatoes, figs, and oranges on the tables of the laboring man the year around. "Altogether," says Wright, "it is a bright new world. It did not exist in their dreams ten years ago."

He goes on to say that young boys who knew only unemployment or wretched poverty are now being trained in vocational schools. Thousands of teenagers are learning plumbing, carpentry, automobile and motor repair, and other trades where they will earn good wages. There has been a flourishing business also for American-made equipment and American school books in the educational program.

As a matter of fact, for the small investment in Latin America, we are now selling to those countries more farm machinery and tools than the money we have invested in these countries in help.

Yet this program is costing the average American taxpayers only *one cent a year!*

Thanks to this small investment, Wright says, myriads of ragged, hitherto half-starved Latin Americans in sixteen republics to the south of the United States, who have been subsisting in misery, are now winning a spectacular new lease on life. They have been cured of malaria and other diseases which for centuries chained them to a subhuman level of existence. They are growing as much as 50 per cent more food on the same acreage. For the first time they are eating nourishing, vitamin-rich meals.

The little farmers are making money as they never did before. They are building clean, solid homes to replace the hovels in which their families have always lived. Their children for the first time are going to school, and the grown-ups are learning how to make more profit from their work and to spend their money more intelligently and helpfully. The farmers now have something to live for. The unhealthiest and poorest and unhappiest, who are easy targets for the communists, have begun to see themselves as members of the property-owning system, and not as its victims. They know that back of their new well-being are North Americans, people from the United States, "Yankees." They are being converted into our friends, friends of the democratic way of life.

Paraguay

In Paraguay, the IIAA has been operating in three ways: improving health and sanitation, increasing the food supply, and promoting education. Here, 65 per cent of the farm population did not own their land, were undernourished, lived in dirty, one-room huts. Now they have a farm credit system copied after that in the United States. Paraguay is turning into a money-making economy. The first thing they did in 1946 was to settle thirty-five families in a pilot colony at Tiroreta, near Asuncion. Each of these families received fifty-seven acres of land on easy payments. IIAA showed them how to lay out their land for money crops providing pasturage for work animals, and vegetable gardens to raise their own food.

Experts tested two thousand types of seeds, adopting over a hundred which were suitable for Paraguay. Now the Paraguayans may all have good seeds.

Albion W. Patterson is one of the men who produced great changes in Paraguay. He introduced a steel plow and a cultivator, and he ran the plow and cultivator himself to show people how it worked, until they gave up the old customs and used the new implements. Patterson went to Paraguay in 1942. He impressed the people there by his constant activity—he seemed to be always in motion, picking up samples of soil, riding on horseback. He didn't dress like a foreign dignitary or business-man. He went about in a soft shirt open at the neck, and always looked as though he were about ready to go to work, or had just come from work. In Latin America, people are judged by their clothes more than people are in the United States, so Patterson was often misjudged.

The government of the United States and the government of Paraguay entered into an agreement to help the farmers and lift their standard of living. Their organization was staffed by Pat-terson and other technicians from the United States. They first trained many Paraguayans to make a census of livestock, and of agricultural conditions. This gave them also a chance to ex-plain to the farmers what they proposed to do. Then a credit organization was started, so that the farmer could get money by borrowing it without going to usurious moneylenders.

Meanwhile, they were doing something for the women. A domestic work-center was established which farm women from the vicinity were invited to join. They were told of improve-ments that could be made. The women brought their young chil-dren with them, and were taught better care of children, and how to train them. A nutrition survey was made of the country, and it was found that the people do not eat enough green vege-tables. So the women were taught how to use these, and how to cook beans, onions, cabbage, and spinach.

Venezuela

In Venezuela, there is a town named San Félix, with thirty-six hundred population. It was malarial. The water was so bad that everybody had dysentery. Then iron ore was found. It always had been there, but the Spanish explorers and all who followed them were chased out by malaria and dysentery. The Institute of Inter-American Affairs began a program of sanitation, digging wells and putting chemicals into the water to purify it. The peo-ple now have sanitary facilities in their homes and can keep their houses clean. They can spray their lawns, wash their streets, and have fire-protection. They are starting small industries and San Félix is beginning to boom.

Fear was one big hindrance to progress among these people, as it is among all backward people. One timid farmer in Venezuela raised a good crop of rice on his three acres, but then he was afraid to store it in his own house, for fear somebody would burn it down. He was also afraid to let the farm agents store it for him, for fear they might never give it back. Finally, the poor little man brought his crop to the farm agent after dark, but he stacked his own bags carefully off by themselves so he could remember which ones they were. The vast majority of the illiterate farmers of the world are tenants. All around the world, unscrupulous landlords have taken the good storage grain from the tenants and substituted poor grain, or have gotten their grain at the lowest possible prices.

In Venezuela, Mr. Nelson Rockefeller conducted two experiments which will be useful to those who are trying to help other countries. As a first experiment, he organized a joint Venezuela-America investors' program, to share the profits as cooperatives do. This helped Venezuela, but it made no money for the investors, and they complained. When people invest for profit, they look for projects which bring dividends. The things that need most to be done seldom bring cash profits.

As a second experiment, he tried a purely philanthropic program called "The American International Association." This has been a great success. His Farm Company has been able to introduce better breeds of cattle into sections of Venezuela. In two cities there are now very successful milk companies which have greatly improved the quality and quantity of milk, and have lowered prices. As a result, the use of milk increased 400 per cent in those areas.

Peru

Thirty agents of IIAA in Peru demonstrated how American know-how could change their country. They wandered along country roads with pruning shears and insecticide sprays, pruning and spraying and clearing away the undergrowth. They persuaded farmers to dig up their old cotton and plant a high-yield variety, with the result that they produced 30 per cent more, and sold it for three times as much money because it was a better variety.

Vocational education in Peru is one of the romances of the IIAA. All the education in Peru in former years had been cultural only, as it was in most of the world. This kind of education qualified them only for clerical jobs of which there weren't enough in the Peruvian government to go around. The new industrial age needed men and women with industrial training. So, since April 1944, IIAA has sent many technical experts to Peru to cooperate with their Ministry of Education in establishing technical training schools. There are 112 technical institutes now, and Peru has only ninety-eight national high schools left to do the old cultural training.

Another revolution in education is the amount of practical laboratory experience now being given the students. In former times, education was wholly theoretical with no practice. For example, an engineer who studied in Peru could get no experience in building a bridge or house or road in his own schools. He would have to go to another country to get that experience. His education had consisted of listening to lectures and reading textbooks, and nothing more. Graduates wore white collars and did not know how to work. But today, technical students in Peru spend half their time in workshops applying what they learn in their classrooms. The government of Peru launched a ten-year plan for improving technical education. Some of the trades now being taught are: craftsmanship in silver, weaving, leathercraft, pottery, carpetmaking, woodcarving, plumbing, house building, auto mechanics, electricity, radio, foundry and pattern-making, forging and welding, and sheet metals.

All of these trades naturally required a new set of textbooks. The first men who were trained in these schools had to translate texts from the English language. Some of the texts they translated are: Heat Treatment of Iron and Steel, Fundamentals of

Mechanical Drawing, Fundamentals of Radio, Bench Mechanics, Industrial Arts Manual, Electric Welding, Course in Dressmaking, Shop Arithmetic. A hundred other books of that nature were also translated from English.

This type of practical aid will command the enthusiastic support of every clear-thinking American businessman. It means closer friendship between North and South America, and an ever-growing opportunity for business and investment among our neighbors to the south.

The IIAA has also greatly aided the farmers of Peru. We speak of the "Irish" potato, but in reality the potato came from the highlands along the Andean slopes. But the soil-worm and various insects had attacked potatoes in Peru, and in many regions wiped them out. So the IIAA (they called it "Servicio Cooperativo") distributed chemicals to destroy the pests, and persuaded farmers to try raising potatoes again.

In 1943, only 2,000 farmers called on this service. But in 1950 there were 47,000 who called on it for help. The use of insecticides resulted in the increase in potato production of more than 100 per cent. In 1946, there were 663,000 tons of potatoes produced; in 1950, over 1,300,000 tons.

Haiti

Haiti is a beautiful country, with wonderful mountains, but it is difficult for her people to make a living. Out of 6.4 million acres, only 2.5 million acres can be used for farming. The weather is too dry most of the time, rains quickly vanish into the limestone, and much of the good soil has been eroded away.

In this needy land the Institute has made fine progress. So great was the problem that at first some of our foreign workers came home saying that it was hopeless. It turned out, however, that all other problems centered in one fundamental need: water. The capital city of Port-au-Prince needed twelve million gallons a day, and it was getting only three million. Major Edwin L. Dudley, sanitary engineer from North Carolina, scrambled around the hills trying to find an abundant supply. Finally he discovered underground springs in sufficient numbers to supply the city with pure water. More than two million gallons are carried daily into the city from one of these underground wells.

A desert of 100,000 acres spread out on both sides of the only big river, the Artibonite. Irrigation canals, dug with bulldozers, changed this desert into a fertile garden. Sixteen miles of irrigation canals resulted in 5,000 acres of new farm land, and the work continues.

Water is one of the most perplexing problems in Latin-American countries, as it is in three-fourths of the world, especially in Asia, Africa, and Australia. Where there is not enough water, people will omit both bathing and laundering. Or, if they do have water, it is likely to be so foul that both bathing and laundering are dangerous. The new water supply of Haiti is changing the habits of her people.

The illiterate people of Haiti have been so frequently swindled that they are suspicious of everybody. They have to be shown! For example, Haitian chickens produced only tiny eggs that would bring 15 cents a dozen. The American agents imported New Hampshire Reds to be distributed among the farmers, but the peasants showed no interest, because it did not look as though their new roosters would be any good in cock fights. But when people saw the size of the eggs the hens laid, everybody wanted them.

One agent brought some new eggplants in, and tried to interest Haitian villagers in growing them, but nobody wanted them. When harvest time came, however, those plants were three times as big as any others they had ever seen and the villagers bought 250,000 of them!

Brazil

The Institute of Inter-American Affairs was very successful in its work in Brazil, where it has excellent cooperation with the government. There are five programs going on in different parts of Brazil, but the one that IIAA is most proud of is in the Rio

Doce valley. This began in 1943, in order to protect the health of laborers who were building a railway, living in camps around Vitoria-Minas. This was during the war, and the railway was being built as fast as possible in order to reach large deposits of iron ore and other strategic materials.

The laborers on this railroad construction died at a fearful rate from dysentery and typhoid fever. The water was bad, and sanitary conditions were terrible. So a very large Brazilian-American health program called SESP (Servicio Especial de Saude Publica) went to work. Fresh water from springs and wells was pumped into reservoirs with hand pumps. The workers covered these reservoirs to keep out disease and dirt and constructed public faucets which every laborer could use. They built individual latrines for each home and chlorinating centers to purify the water were installed. A campaign was started against mosquitoes, for it was found that 50 per cent of the workers had malaria.

Special attention was given to the health of the women and children of the laborers. Dental clinics took care of the teeth of both children and adults. Sanitary inspectors could go around to homes, hotels, restaurants, schools, and markets and correct any unsanitary condition they found. Disease and deaths fell off tremendously, production increased, and the people were happy. That railroad has long since been finished, but the social work begun among those laborers has continued to spread until it is all over Brazil.

The IIAA in Brazil has benefited the United States. American and European capitalists now have $600 million invested in Brazil, and Brazilian companies have added $2 billion to their own capital.

Brazil's per capita income is now four times the world average, but it is less than one-fourth of the per capita income of the United States. Life expectancy in Brazil is still only thirty-nine years. As her health and economic conditions improve, Brazil will become an ever more wonderful neighbor for the United States.

Bolivia

In Bolivia, on the high plateaus of the Andes mountains, live about five million Kechua and Aymara Indians. They were about the most wretched human beings I had ever seen, many of them being addicted to a drug called hemp, which makes them lazy and stupid. They are now undergoing a great change. The Institute of Inter-American Affairs is trying to lift them out of their poverty.

Charlotte Thompson went as a nurse to the Bolivian town of Cochabamba. She found the most primitive kind of homes, with no light, fresh air, or heat, and walls and floors of mud. In a year she had trained eight nurses who knew the Kechua language as well as Spanish. While the Bolivian nurses were helping Miss Thompson, they kept explaining: "You can't do things that way here. You don't know our people. They will never change."

They zoned the city, and the nurses went out timidly, because in Bolivia no señorita walks the streets alone. They took a census to determine health conditions and to inform the people that they could get treatment. Within a year, 6,562 attended their clinic. Three years later 47,000 had taken advantage of this service.

To carry on the health program, the Institute has in each country an organization called a "Servicio," which is training an army of people in public sanitation.

Servicios now have 160 hospitals and health centers, twelve schools of nursing, four graduate schools of sanitary engineering, three graduate schools of public health. About thirteen hundred men and women have come to the United States to receive postgraduate training in medicine and public health. Besides roundworm and hookworm, the common diseases that bother everybody in the tropics are malaria, yellow fever, smallpox, typhus, yaws, and a skin disease called "mal de pintos." DDT has become a great friend of Latin America, for it is the most potent enemy of mosquitoes and lice, which spread disease.

The *Farm Commerce Weekly* said, in April of 1951, that the activities of the Institute of Inter-American Affairs were estimated to have affected directly or indirectly one-half of the population of Latin America. That population is 157,000,000 people, almost the same as the population of the United States.

While hundreds of men and women like Charlotte Thompson were out on the battle line, the major credit for the success of the IIAA must go to Nelson Rockefeller. When histories are written many people receive more credit than they deserve, but Nelson Rockefeller is self-effacing and will probably receive less credit in history than he should. Being a very rich man, he finds it necessary to protect himself from hordes of people who are after his money, just as all rich people do. This has kept him even more out of the limelight. So it is a pleasure to pay tribute to a millionaire who has the true conception of philanthropy and who has hewn away at his idea until, more than any other one man, he has been a benefactor to all Latin America. Today, South America gives us less worry than any other continent. It serves as our best illustration of the wisdom of putting Christ's way of compassion into practice.

Today, when we are troubled at the threats of communism and hydrogen bombs and intercontinental missiles in the Eastern Hemisphere, we are not afraid of our neighbors in the Western Hemisphere, although they touch us on both the north and the south. Why is not Latin America a threat to us? It was a threat until Herbert Hoover, during his presidency, paid a visit to Latin America and started the "good neighbor" policy. He was followed by Franklin D. Roosevelt, in whose administration the Institute of Inter-American Affairs was begun. There can be no shadow of doubt that this "good neighbor policy" has made Latin America our friend.

Every far-sighted American regrets now that we did not long ago start a good neighbor program for the whole world. Alas we did not start it for Asia and Africa until 1950, with Point Four. But at least we can learn from our mistakes, and continue those programs which are really helping people to help themselves.

The Institute of Inter-American Affairs has served as a splendid example for the work now being undertaken throughout the world by the United States and by the United Nations.

CHAPTER 13

HOW THE UNITED NATIONS BEGAN— AND THE WORLD BANK

In 1943, DURING WORLD WAR II, THERE CAME INTO BEING AT Atlantic City an organization with a long name—"The United Nations Relief and Rehabilitation Administration" (UNRRA for short). Its purpose was to aid the areas stricken by war, where people were without proper food, clothing, shelter, and medical care. UNRRA worked on both sides of the Iron Curtain, and some of its best technicians came from the USSR and its satellites.

UNRRA had no precedent to guide it, and, although it was motivated by high ideals, it made some big mistakes. All pioneers make mistakes—they are blazing a trail, have no guideposts, and cannot always see where they are ultimately going. It is so much the fashion to condemn UNRRA for these mistakes that there is need for a word in its defense. When one adds both sides of the ledger, it did far more good than harm. UNRRA was not the only organization which wasted money and made mistakes in those hectic days. It was incomparably less wasteful than the war itself!

UNRRA had to work quickly, and it was forced to employy

many men who were not properly qualified but who were the best it could get. No doubt there was a waste of time, talent and money; yet in spite of all this, millions of people *were* saved from starvation, the homeless *were* given homes, and almost three billion dollars' worth of food was shipped from fortunate countries to the devastated areas. By the aid of UNRRA, many industries were started again.

While UNRRA does not deserve to be criticized for corruption within its own organization, it does deserve criticism because it was not tough enough in dealing with corrupt profiteers in the receiving countries. It did not start black markets, but it permitted them. These black marketeers got materials for little or nothing and sold them for 1000 per cent or more profit.

One Filipino wrote me that "We had hoped that UNRRA would heal the wounds of this terrible war, but instead it has broken our hearts." I know what he meant, for I saw the black markets on the streets of Manila, selling to the poor people what we had meant to give them. Millions of Americans were disgusted by the black markets which they saw in many countries. They had given their money to help feed the hungry, and saw it used to make scoundrels rich. The weakness of UNRRA was that it had not planned for sufficient control over materials after they reached needy countries.

We are incomparably richer for what UNRRA tried to do, and we have gained much, even by their early mistakes. One thing we have learned is that, while money is necessary to do a job, it is not as important as the integrity and ability of the people who are sent abroad to spend it. We have learned from UNRRA that it is not enough to do the right thing. It must be done in the right spirit, by people with the right heart!

The share of the United States in UNRRA was $2,300,000,000.

UNRRA ceased to exist in June, 1945. The work which it started was continued by many important organizations, which are best known by their alphabetical names, UN, WHO, FAO, UNESCO, and UNICEF.

The United Nations came into being in San Francisco, October 24, 1945. That date will henceforth be to the world what July 4, 1776 is to the United States.

"WE, THE PEOPLES OF THE UNITED NATIONS, DETERMINED . . . to save succeeding generations from the scourge of war. . . ." This is the great objective with which the United Nations opens its charter.

To end war and all causes of war! That means to end the things that make men feel unjustly treated, that make men fear, that make men hate, that make men want to fight and kill. It means fighting the hunger which makes men desperate, and the disease which makes men see red. It means fighting the ignorance which leaves them helpless victims of exploitation.

Literature about the United Nations is excellent, clear, and easily obtained. In this book we are interested in its programs of compassion. For the first time in human history, more than seventy of the nations of the world have united in an effort to lift humanity out of destitution and despair, up to a new level of hope and progress. It is the first truly world-wide fulfillment of the compassionate purpose of Jesus, when He said, "The Spirit of the Lord is upon me, because he hath anointed me to preach the gospel to the poor; he hath sent me to heal the broken-hearted, to preach deliverance to the captives, and recovering of sight to the blind, to set at liberty them that are bruised."

There are six main divisions in the United Nations:

1. The General Assembly—*All* the member nations.
2. The Security Council—Eleven countries, of whom six change every two years. They are supposed to keep the peace by nipping incipient wars in the bud.
3. The Economic and Social Council—Eighteen nations, six elected each year for three-year terms. This is the organization which performs many of the deeds of compassion, more than any other branch of the United Nations. *It is the hope of the underprivileged world.*
4. The Trusteeship Council—Has had control of such backward areas as eastern New Guinea. It will grow less and less important, as more lands achieve freedom.
5. The International Court of Justice—Fifteen judges. It ought to grow more important as years go by.

6. The Secretariat—The Secretary-General, Dag Hammarskjold of Sweden, has the hardest job, keeping the UN going, keeping it together, and carrying out its commands.

Of all its six divisions, the Economic and Social Council is the one in which this book is most interested, because the compassion of the United Nations flows through it.

Under this Economic and Social Council are several subdivisions so wonderful in their objectives that they make the heart sing. But they also make the head reel, for they have a dizzy array of alphabetical names. We will need to get acquainted with some of these if we hope to realize what good they are doing in the world.

Over 900,000 Arab refugees fled out of Israel when it became a republic. For nearly ten years, these refugees from Palestine have been living in camps, one-third of them in tents secured from army surplus. The refugees are unaccustomed to living in tents, which are fearfully hot in summer and cold in winter.

The United Nations Relief and Works Agency (UNRWA), not to be confused with UNRRA, spends $28 million a year just to feed the refugees. During the year ending June 30, 1956, the United States government contributed $16,700,000 of this sum.

These refugees constitute one of the best breeding grounds for communism in the whole world. All the elements on which communism thrives are present—physical destitution, deteriorating morale, disgust with their old leaders, doubts about the motives of the West, unemployment, idleness, frustration, and an almost hopeless future. Communism is outlawed, so there is little open mention of it. But communist slogans are spoken everywhere.

The average monthly ration the refugees receive from the United Nations consists of the following, for each person: twenty-two pounds of flour, a pound of sugar, a pound and five ounces of dried vegetables, one pound and two ounces of rice, five ounces of margarine, nine ounces of oil, and three and a half ounces of soap. This monthly ration costs $1.85 per person! It is supposed to provide each refugee with a daily diet of 1500 calories. There is no meat, milk, butter or cheese, no eggs, fresh vegetables, or fruits.

Generally, the refugees use up this monthly ration after twenty-five days. After that they gather herbs and tree roots and cactus plants. Some of them get a little work, but their pay is seldom more than the equivalent of 20 cents a day.

Their hardest time is in the winter, when employment is almost at a complete standstill. It is very cold in the winter, and the lack of warm clothing then is worse even than the scarcity of food. After five years of exile, most of these refugees have nothing of their own left but rags. They have to rely upon contributions from voluntary agencies such as the Lutheran World Federation, the Pontifical Mission of Palestine, Church World Service, the Congregational Christian Service Committee, and the American Middle East Relief. These are trying to supply adequate clothing for nearly a million persons.

The United Nations Medical Service is fairly successful in preventing any serious outbreaks of cholera, typhus or bubonic plague, but less successful with dysentery, which is very common. Fifty per cent of the people are also suffering with eye disease, due primarily to the flies. A campaign has been waged against these flies, and also against lice and fleas, with which nearly 40 per cent of the people are infested.

Fifty per cent of all these refugees are under sixteen years of age! That figure reveals how tragically the older people have perished, unable to endure the hardships of the crowded camps. These 400,000 young people are growing up under very unwholesome conditions, and have a sadly distorted view of life. United Nations, through UNESCO, has opened schools for nearly all the small children.

The idle life which these refugees lead makes them sluggish. They sleep away the hours of the meaningless days. Many have lost self-respect and self-confidence, and are unwilling to take any risk when a job is offered them. Everywhere one finds bitterness among them. They are bitter against all the Western powers, who they claim are responsible for their misery; and they are bitter against the United Nations for not doing more. They are even bitter against the Arab countries, which they say sold out to the Jews.

Along with their bitterness is wide distrust, which makes it unpleasant to work with them. They have opposed any plan for re-settlement because they want to return to their own homes in Israel. They say, "We are ready to live twenty years under these tents rather than give up the right of going home where we belong."

UNRWA has one of the hardest jobs in the world.

The World Bank

The International Bank for Reconstruction and Development (IBRD), is an essential part of the program of redeeming the world from poverty. None of the largest programs could take place without it. So useful is the IBRD that it has been called a "rescue mission for the nations."

The World Bank was organized in 1944 at a conference at Bretton Woods, New Hampshire; twenty-eight nations signed Articles of Agreement in December, 1945, in Washington, D.C. It now has sixty members.

Where did the Bank get its money? Every member nation put in an amount based on its wealth and trade. The United States, with half the world's wealth, subscribed the largest share, $3,175,000,000. Little Panama put in $200,000. The other nations were in between these two extremes, the total amount subscribed being over $9 billion. The countries pay into the Bank only 20 per cent of the amounts they subscribed. The rest they guarantee, when and if it is needed.

This money is loaned to aid reconstruction and improvement projects. The Bank can lend to any of its sixty member governments, or to any private concern inside a country if that country's government guarantees to back the private company.

It loans only if it finds a worthy and important cause which may fail for want of capital. Frequently, private banks assume a large part of a loan, and the Bank carries the remainder. But it will not loan its money if the borrower can get the money anywhere else.

The Bank began by loaning money in 1947 to the war-tattered nations of Europe, France, the Netherlands, Denmark, and Luxembourg, to buy supplies of food and clothing from North America. But a year later, the Marshall Plan was started by the United States. As the countries could then get money, the Bank discontinued its lending to Europe for that purpose.

The International Bank will not loan the money to any country unless it is convinced that the country needs it to purchase foreign supplies, and that proper use will be made of the money. The more helpful the project seems to be, the more likely the country is to get the money. The borrowing country must have the knowledge and financial position to carry the enterpise on to success. And of course the Bank will not loan any money unless there is a reasonable prospect that the loan will be repaid.

Many little countries took advantage of this opportunity to borrow money. To El Salvador, in Central America, the Bank loaned $12 million to build a dam and a hydroelectric power plant on the Lempa River. This will double that country's electric power supply, stimulate economic expansion, provide irrigation, and give lights to homes all over El Salvador.

The Bank loaned $24 million in 1949 to Mexico, and some of this was used to purchase a small diesel power plant to generate electricity in the town of Tecuala, on the west coast. In three years' time there were some striking results of that loan, as reported by the Bank: "Industrial users of electricity in Tecuala have risen from just three to thirty-three; the town has acquired a public library, a daily newspaper, a radio station, and a night school. Tecuala's population has trebled, and the number of students in its schools has increased seven times."

The mayor of Tecuala recently said, "I have witnessed our emergence from the dark ages into an age of light."

The Bank loaned India $139 million in 1950. Of this, $118 million was for the tremendous Damovar Dam, which is modeled on America's Tennessee Valley Project. Also, $31.5 million was loaned to India for use in improving the Indian Iron and Steel Company.

One of the four most stupendous undertakings in international projects of our time was to have been the Aswan Dam on the Nile River. The entire project would have cost about $1.3 billion. Of this, the Egyptian government proposed to provide $940 million in labor, materials and money. The International Bank offered to loan Egypt $200 million if the United States or some other country would loan about $70 million more.

Late in 1955, the governments of the United States and the United Kingdom announced that they were sympathetic toward financing the Dam, along with the World Bank. Two months later, the World Bank announced that substantial agreement had been reached concerning the basis of the Bank's participation, in an amount equivalent to $200 million. The Bank issued the statement: "There do not appear to be any alternative investment opportunities of equal promise. Without Sadd-el Aali [the Aswan Dam], the growth in the economy [of Egypt] is likely to lag much behind the probable increase in the population. This would mean a steady decline in the standard of living, with serious implications for the future social and political evolution of the country. . . ."

What would the Dam make possible for Egypt's hungry multitudes? Its reservoir would store 70 billion cubic meters of water for irrigation. It could hold 30 billion cubic meters for flood control, and would have 30 billion of storage for silt control. It would increase the farm land by one-third. The country's agricultural income would be increased ultimately by nearly half! Floods would be controlled, enabling farmers to raise more than one crop a year. It would also greatly facilitate getting crops to market, for navigation of the Nile River would be stable throughout the year.

The electric generating capacity of Egypt would increase from 540,000 kilowatts to about 1,900,000.

Here are a very few of the statistics on the Aswan High Dam Project: the Dam would be 361 feet in height; 3.1 miles in length, and 4,276 feet thick at its base. It would dwarf the Pyramids!

A press release of February, 1956 read: "It is the opinion of the Western negotiators and of diplomats in Cairo that the Egyptians are completely sincere in declaring that they would by far prefer the West's assistance to that of the East."

But the participation of the United States in the project was brought to an abrupt end by the announcement of John Foster Dulles on July 19, 1956, that "America is no longer interested."

It is true that Egypt had been making tremendous purchases of arms from Russia and Yugoslavia with money which the United States thought was needed for the Dam.

A full discussion of the merits of this problem is beyond the scope of this book. But the importance of the Dam for the progress of Egypt is beyond question.

In all, forty-four countries have thus far borrowed from the World Bank $2,858,000,000 for such projects as electric power, agriculture, coal mining, iron and steel, telephone equipment, railroads and highways, harbors, wood-product industries, radio transmission, flood control, aircraft, gas pipelines, and grain storage facilities. It is altogether possible that the World Bank will prove to be among the greatest boons of all time to the human race.

CHAPTER 14

꧁ ꧂

WORLD HEALTH ORGANIZATION
AND
UNITED NATIONS CHILDREN'S FUND

CHOLERA BROKE OUT IN CAIRO IN 1947, JUST AS MOSLEM PIL-
grims began flooding through Egypt toward Mecca. This deadly
scourge of the ages, which had often killed a million in a few
weeks, had again reached out its hand to claim another multitude! But this time the world was ready! At once, Aly Tewfik
Shousha of the Ministry of Health in Cairo threw a cordon of
soldiers around the infected canals where people were throwing
the bodies of the dead cholera victims.

Talking from New York City by long distance telephone, Dr.
Frank Calderone of WHO (World Health Organization of the
UN) got from American druggists all the anti-cholera vaccine
he could find. Two large Philadelphia firms offered vaccine at
the price fixed by the government. This was rushed by motor
trucks at seventy miles an hour to La Guardia Airport in New
York City. At the request of the Mayor of New York City, the
city contributed a huge supply of syringes. A million sulfaguani-
dine tablets were obtained from the United States War Assets
Administration. Fourteen countries sent anti-cholera vaccine,

thirty-two *tons* of it, to Cairo, and practically everybody in Egypt was vaccinated.

Within three months the epidemic was whipped. There had been 20,000 cases and 10,000 had died. It was estimated that the World Health Organization had saved from 50,000 to 100,000 lives.

Before that epidemic was conquered, the American Congress had been opposing our participation in WHO. But by the time the epidemic ended Congress had changed its mind, and in September of 1948, WHO became officially a specialized agency of the United Nations with the approval of the United States.

Thanks to WHO, it had been possible *for the first time in history to mobilize the whole wide world's resources to end an epidemic.* Now, WHO has an epidemic service with world-wide broadcasting facilities, so that if an epidemic breaks out it can be crushed or isolated. This is fortunate, for now with airplanes going everywhere and people traveling around the world in great numbers, the plague, or typhus, or yellow fever could easily spread everywhere in a few weeks.

The goal of WHO around the globe is more than to cure people who are ill—it is to stop disease in its tracks, and drive it from the face of the earth! That first wonderful victory over cholera in Egypt came within a year after its organization. WHO could hardly have been born at a more timely hour in history!

The World Health Organization began in July, 1946. It included sixty-four nations, thirteen of which were not in the United Nations. Its purpose was stated thus: "The attainment, by all peoples, of the highest possible level of health. . . ."

WHO is vast. It coordinates health work in a hundred countries now. By working with Rockefeller medical programs, with mission hospitals, and with many governments, World Health Organization has already performed miracles in health improvement. By the end of this century, the biggest problem will not be health, but how to feed those who will then be alive.

One of WHO's most spectacular successes is against malaria, which strikes 300 million people a year. In Indonesia alone, 30 million are infected. Ten per cent of all deaths in the world are due to malaria. WHO has been battling malaria in Afghanistan, India, Pakistan, Thailand and other countries. It joined other agencies in a mass attack on malaria in Greece, and in parts of Greece cut malaria down from 80 per cent of the population to 5 per cent. As a result, food production there rose as much as 70 per cent, and the income of families increased from $196 to $358 annually.

Even the richest soil can be virtually worthless if it breeds the mosquito that makes the farmer too sick to harvest his crops. *That is the tragic story behind hundreds of millions of acres of good land on every continent that have not been producing: the farmers were too sick to plant or reap.*

One of the striking instances of how malaria can be defeated comes from north India, a land that urgently needs more productive land to feed her 400 million people. In 1950, one and a half million acres of potentially fertile land in the Himalayan foothills was a jungle swamp because of malaria. Seventy-seven out of a hundred children were victims of the disease. Today, as a result of combined efforts of three agencies of the United Nations—WHO, UNICEF, and FAO—the mosquito has been wiped out. Already, 40,000 acres of this malaria-free land are under cultivation by families who were refugees from Pakistan, and the production of food grains has risen by 30 per cent. But most heartwarming is the news that only three out of a hundred children had malaria there this year, a drop of 96 per cent in four years! DDT is now protecting 105 million people in India from this disease.

Two United Nations agencies, WHO and UNICEF, fight malaria in Asia, Africa, Latin America and the Middle East by starting anti-malaria campaigns. UNICEF, described on page 140, provides the equipment such as DDT, sprayers, laboratories for malaria research, and other supplies. WHO furnishes the doctors and trains the local malaria workers. The governments, after they are given this start by the UN groups, are continuing to fight malaria on their own power. To insure them a cheap, local supply of DDT permanently, local factories are built to manufacture it. Near Cairo there is a plant that will produce enough DDT in its first six months of operation to pay for the entire cost of its installation.

WHO has also set out to conquer venereal disease, especially syphilis. Fifty per cent of the population of some parts of eastern Africa are infected by this malady. WHO is now fighting both gonorrhea and syphilis with the wonder drug, penicillin.

A newsletter of WHO's activities is issued bi-monthly, and it may be obtained for the asking. This newsletter describes how the World Health Organization is warring on the three greatest disease scourges of the human race: malaria, tuberculosis, and venereal disease.

It is also waging war on more than thirty other world diseases. Among these are leprosy, typhus, polio, diphtheria, trachoma, rabies, anthrax, Q-fever, and bilharziasis. This last disease is the curse of millions in Egypt. It is a parasite that is carried about by a snail, and enters persons through their feet. Like hookworm, bilharziasis does not kill those who are infected, but it robs them of health and energy. Very recently a drug has been developed to combat this disease.

United Nations Children's Fund (UNICEF)

UNICEF was organized in 1946. It stands for mercy to the "littlest and least" of the children of the world. The name of the agency was originally United Nations International Children's Emergency Fund, but was changed in 1953. UNICEF remains as the symbol.

One thing is certain—every child whom we permit to come into the world has a right to "life, liberty, and the pursuit of happiness," and therefore to health. Good health and happiness are twins. If the problem of overpopulation must be faced, it can find a solution in family planning, but never in killing off people or allowing them to be killed off by disease, hunger, and war! Today we realize clearly that we cannot permit them "to die and so decrease the surplus population," as Dickens' Scrooge recommended in *A Christmas Carol*. That would be murdering the innocent by our neglect.

The underdeveloped countries, with more than half of the world's children, have a terrific mortality rate among babies. In these countries fifty to three hundred out of every thousand babies are dead when they are born! Life expectancy is only about thirty years. In the worst areas, half the children are dead before their tenth year. Contrast that with Sweden, where only two babies out of every hundred die in the first year of their lives, and the life expectancy is seventy years.

UNICEF is already producing a great change in many countries. In Pacoti, Brazil, a priest pointed to his church steeple and said to a visitor from UNICEF: "The bell used to toll the death of a baby three or four times a day. Now it tolls only three or four times a month. That is what UNICEF has meant to Pacoti."

The list of tragic mistakes made by midwives in backward areas is long and horrible. UNICEF is helping governments train a new army of midwives who will know the simple, necessary things to do to save mothers and their babies.

It was a real triumph for UNICEF in Afghanistan when two daughters of the Prime Minister enrolled in the midwifery school in Kabul. In rigidly Moslem Afghanistan, women are never seen except by their families, behind walls. They are completely veiled when on the street. The courageous step on the part of the Prime Minister and his daughters represented a violent change in social custom. It meant the beginning of a revolution in the attitude of the Afghans toward their women.

UNICEF attacks the diseases of children with three powerful modern weapons: first, with BCG, a vaccine against tuberculosis; second, with DDT, used against malaria, typhus, and other insect-carried diseases; and third, with penicillin, used against yaws and syphilis.

Yaws is the most common disease in less developed countries. It covers children, as well as older people, with sores like boils, even on the soles of their feet and the palms of their hands, so that the victims can neither walk nor work. It is far more contagious and persistent than leprosy, and far more common. It is more horrible to look at than leprosy, and if untreated is even more disastrous. Its victims do not die, but drag out an increasingly painful existence, with the bones being eaten away, as termites eat up old wood. In Indonesia alone, there are around ten million people with yaws. Penicillin is the miracle cure. *One dose only half as large as that used for syphilis is needed!*

UNICEF and WHO work hand in hand in many countries. The World Health Organization sends experts out to give instructions. UNICEF provides the medicine, the equipment, and the jeeps to carry the workers.

This is what they are doing in Indonesia: the Indonesian government has provided personnel, buildings, and equipment worth more than all the combined UN agency contributions. Nearly four hundred small medical teams, trained by the WHO experts, jeeped along narrow, rutted trails, or traveled by foot, going from village to village, examining 750,000 persons a month for yaws. The headman brought all his people together, explaining what was to be done; and the villagers lined up for diagnosis. When telltale sores were spotted on a child, he got a shot of penicillin—fifteen cents' worth! That cures even the worst case. A child whose body is covered with open sores will, a month later, have only scars as evidence of his past suffering. Happily, the cost of penicillin is constantly being reduced and as a result, seven times as many cases can be treated for the same money as could be cured only four years ago.

In eight years, UNICEF has helped treat over six million victims of yaws in Indonesia alone. One farmer told what this meant to him: "Six months ago, I was suffering from yaws and could not work. My wife and children were hungry. My rice fields had not been planted for more than a year. I had sold my only buffalo."

When the penicillin men came to the village, this farmer was first in line for an injection, and here is the result: "After one month, all my sores disappeared. I gained back my strength and planted my rice field. Next month we are harvesting our paddy."

In one village in Java a big feast was held in honor of penicillin and UNICEF, and the newly cured men and women danced for joy.

Gradually, this great crusade of the United Nations against yaws is spreading over the world, reaching the stricken people of India, the Philippines, Malaya, Fiji, Western Samoa, Thailand, Haiti, Bechuanaland, Liberia and Nigeria, where nearly 50 per cent of the rural people are infected.

UNICEF has already treated about 40 per cent of the estimated cases in the world. At the present rate it will take only a few more years to bring yaws under complete control.

UNICEF and WHO have teamed up also against tuberculosis. In Asia, this disease is called the "quiet death." It is not like the sudden death of cholera, which kills in hours, or the living death of yaws, which cripples and disfigures but is seldom fatal. Tuberculosis might well also be called the "creeping death," for it works secretly and relentlessly. It has already marked for early doom one person in every thirty in India, where it kills 500,000 a year. It thrives on poverty. England now has only thirty tuberculosis cases per 100,000 population. India has 300 per 100,000. Besides the half-million Indians who were dying from it each year, two and a half million more had infectious cases. Two years ago, tuberculosis was the most hopeless and dreaded disease in India. Now, the new BCG vaccination is being used by India and, when combined with a better diet, it promises to conquer this disease, although it is not a miraculous, swift cure like that for yaws.

About 800,000 persons are being inoculated every month. If India had attempted to cure these cases alone, it would have cost her a billion dollars, which is equal to the entire budget of the Indian government. But in this campaign, India is being assisted by UN's health agencies and UNICEF. There are many difficulties to be overcome. The hardships of travel are very great, and the young doctors and technicians have to accept a gypsy life. But UNICEF supplies them with all the things they need. A doctor for WHO said, "Accomplishments already prove that it is possible to plan health programs for all of India's 360 million inhabitants."

The United Nations campaign around the world against tuberculosis is probably the most dramatic effort in the history of man's unremitting struggle to control his ills. Over 170 million people, mostly children, were tested for tuberculosis in Asia alone. In one year 42 million were tested, and 14 million were vaccinated. The UN is also attacking tuberculosis in the Eastern Mediterranean, Africa and Latin America. This global effort is literally the only hope for controlling tuberculosis, which kills one person somewhere every seven seconds.

UNICEF and WHO, working in close cooperation, are spreading out across vast areas, endeavoring to vaccinate everyone in danger of infection, in those countries cooperating in the program. They supply the millions of dollars' worth of essential motor transport, medical supplies, and equipment. Hundreds of teams of technicians have been organized, trained, and sent out.

The vaccine used, Bacillus Calmette Guerin, is called BCG for short. It was developed nearly fifty years ago in France. It does not cure, but it helps prevent tuberculosis. When accompanied by simple sanitary precautions it can probably immunize eight out of ten children vaccinated with it, and those who do contract TB after being vaccinated almost invariably have it in milder form.

The four simple sanitary precautions which must be taken to keep infected people from spreading the disease in their own families are repeated over and over again. "Burn all sputum, air bedclothes daily, let sunlight enter the rooms, and keep the family away from the tubercular person."

The job of bringing TB under control is so stupendous that it would have been hopeless before the UN was organized. But this year, UNICEF and WHO spearhead the efforts of twenty-six governments that are cooperating with great success, and the end of tuberculosis may be prophesied with confidence.

There is no way to give an adequate impression of the vastness of UNICEF's world deeds of compassion without leaving the reader dazed with too much material and too many figures. For example, in remote and primitive Borneo, where there are no roads and few doctors, if people have to go to a hospital they have to travel on rivers, sometimes for a week. The children's wards are everywhere crowded, and the government has small funds for medicine. Mrs. Margueritte Harmon Bro tells how she looked into the kitchen in one of these hospitals and asked the doctor how on earth the children could get well on the food she saw. The doctor said with a grin: "They don't. But look here!" He led her to a large storeroom full of cases of powdered milk, all provided by UNICEF.

For the children of the Belgian Congo, thousands of cans of powdered skim milk are carried on the heads of bearers along footpaths to every village, for most Congo villages have no roads.

In the highlands of Bolivia, typhus, carried by a louse, thrives, and kills one out of every eight of those it attacks. Here, as well as in parts of Afghanistan, UNICEF workers equipped with DDT go from house to house destroying the lice.

Eleanor Roosevelt said in *See* magazine, January, 1953:

Five hundred million children of our world live and die in want. They may never have tasted milk or visited a doctor, but they are very familiar with hunger, cold, and diseases. The only organization that even begins to answer their need is UNICEF. UNICEF has spent about thirty million dollars in six years, and spent it on problems of the needy children of the world. Its total expenditure in six years has been less than the cost of *one* aircraft carrier.

One hundred and fifteen countries have asked UNICEF for assistance, and 104 of them are still receiving aid. When the work under way is completed, untold millions will have been helped. Each country cooperates by furnishing manpower, while UNICEF contributes supplies of all kinds, and experts to train the nationals. It is one of the most efficient organizations on earth, when you count the number of children helped for each dollar spent.

This is what UNICEF says it can do with a dollar: give enough cod liver oil capsules to protect thirteen children for a month against rickets; or give 72 children a glass of milk for seven days; or give enough BCG vaccine to immunize 100 children against tuberculosis; or buy enough penicillin to treat twenty children for yaws; or buy enough DDT to safeguard eight people against malarial mosquitoes for a whole year.

The great problem UNICEF faces is its budget. In 1953 we gave it only $9.8 million; in 1954 we gave only $8.3 million; in 1955 only $9 million. In 1956, we gave $9.7 million. We have been too pinch-penny toward an organization that is doing a unique and successful task.

Fortunately, the underdeveloped countries are themselves contributing more and more. In 1952, they contributed $2 million, which was 17 per cent of the total for that year. They gave this directly to UNICEF, *in addition* to the amounts they spent locally for their children's care. In Viet-Nam, UNICEF invested $40,000, while the hard-pressed government there invested $850,000! Pakistan, although very short of funds, raised $45,000 for UNICEF from private donations.

It is safe to say that no organization in the world receives greater appreciation than UNICEF does, from the people it blesses.

CHAPTER 15

~~~~~~~~~~~~~~~~~~~~~~~

FOOD AND AGRICULTURE ORGANIZATION (FAO) AND UNITED NATIONS EDUCATIONAL, SCIENTIFIC AND CULTURAL ORGANIZATION (UNESCO)

FAO

THE DIVISION OF THE UNITED NATIONS CALLED FOOD AND AGRI-culture Organization began in 1946. It deserves a high place in the story of compassion. In ten years it has done many wonderful things to help solve the hunger problem of the world by teaching people how to produce more food.

To see it working we will visit the little republic of Haiti. The Haitian government asked FAO to develop their fish industry. So FAO set up experimental breeding ponds and stocked streams with fish from Jamaica and the United States. At the same time, a Haitian was sent to Indonesia to study the Indonesian methods of "growing fish." In that country newly hatched carp are thrown into the flooded rice fields, where the tiny fish and the rice grow together. When the fields are drained, the carp are big enough to eat. The Indonesians, living as they do on many islands, are experts at raising fish in closed-in fish ponds by the seashore and in swamps. This art is now being transported by FAO to Haiti and many other countries. It is a fine illustration of the policy FAO has of sharing the secrets of one nation to help feed the people of other lands. Some day we shall recognize that the highest morality is to share the collective wisdom of the race for the benefit of all.

India is another good illustration of FAO in action. She needed to increase her rice production, so FAO started a study of Japanese rice culture, because Japan produced three times as much rice per acre as India did. But FAO found the Japanese rice did not thrive in India with its hot climate. So FAO experts set to work developing a hybrid that would have the high production of the Japanese rice and the heat resistance of the Indian rice; eventually they are sure to find it. Probably this discovering and distributing of hybrid rice throughout the Far East is the most important single program that FAO carries on. The knowledge they are spreading is blessing Asia just as the discovery of hybrid corn has blessed America and Europe.

FAO spent only $40,000 to spread American hybrid corn through Europe, but this added $24 million to the value of Europe's annual corn crop.[1] That is $2 million more than the entire annual investment of the United Nations for the whole world!

The beautiful thing about FAO is that it is a *partnership*. Every nation is giving to every other nation what skills it has to contribute. One hundred and four countries have given either money, or experts, or facilities for study.

FAO now serves an immense territory with scientific help in producing more food. It has established regional training centers in many countries, where students can study food problems in their own language and on the spot, just where help is needed. Technicians are being sent wherever their skills are useful: to Liberia go fisheries experts; to Saudi Arabia goes an engineering survey; to India goes a fertilizing expert; to Ethiopia goes a team

[1] *New York Times,* December 9, 1953.

to establish an agricultural school; to Libya goes a wool-grading expert.

FAO holds an annual conference, where the world food situation is reviewed by leading technical experts from fifty-eight countries. There are also many local training courses where twenty to sixty trainees are prepared for service, through lectures and practical demonstrations. One such training course was held in Marseilles by FAO and WHO, with the French government acting as host. Twenty-six trainees came, half of them from French overseas territories, and half from Spanish, Portuguese, and Italian areas. Some of these trainees went with a nutrition expert to Central America and Panama to study how to improve the diet of the people, since "hidden hunger," caused by not eating a balanced diet, is one of the world's chief problems.

In another training center in North India, at Dehra Dun, the Forest Research Institute trains the students in woodworking, in many types of timber engineering, and in preserving trees from termites and decay. Training centers have been set up also to teach people how to fight forest fires. Others study how to produce pulp for paper, for, as literacy spreads, the need for paper is bound to rise. In Australia, a conference was held to study the use of eucalyptus trees, which grow rapidly in areas too dry for most trees.

In Pakistan, Israel, Saudi Arabia and Syria, FAO engineers are helping with agriculture and the problems of irrigation and drinking water. Securing a sufficient water supply for drinking and irrigation is becoming an ever more difficult problem in four countries out of five. There is no simple answer; in fact, supplying water has become one of the highly expert sciences. In Iran, a team of UN experts is finding water by photographing from the air; in one area they selected fifty-two new sites for wells.

In several countries, FAO experts are showing the farmers how to use hoes, forks, and hay rakes! In some underdeveloped countries, they have never used any of these things. In Afghanistan and Libya, blacksmiths are being trained to make these tools.

When FAO was only ten years old, it had already helped ninety-seven countries and territories with its highly qualified experts. Surprisingly, these experts have come from sixty-four different countries. These have gone not only from the highly developed to the less developed countries, as one might suppose, but also from one underdeveloped country to another. There has been a healthy interchange. India has furnished eighty-four experts to other countries while she has received 136 experts from abroad. She sent 105 fellowship-holders to study in other countries, while ninety-three fellowship-holders came from other countries to India. Brazil too has been a true give-and-take country. It has received thirty-six foreign experts, and sent twenty Brazilian experts to other countries. It sent eighty-six Brazilians with fellowships to other countries to learn, while, on the other hand, 160 foreigners came to Brazil with fellowships. That illustrates how all the world is growing richer by this cross-fertilization of ideas.

Experts were sent to Thailand by the FAO to show the Thais how pineapples are raised as a year-round crop in the Canary Islands. This year, Thailand is raising a year-round crop of pineapples for the first time.

FAO imported tractors into India. By the use of 270 tractors, they plowed 750,000 acres of former waste land, at a cost of $7.5 million. That acreage is now producing wheat which would cost India $36 million to import!

In 1953, FAO began to send technicians to Greece; and that year Greece, in cooperation with the American government, showed the highest production she had ever known. It was the first time in many years that the Greeks had enough rice, beans, and peas, and more than enough olive oil. That country has benefited by technical cooperation for seven years. Four hundred trained experts are now working directly with Greek farmers and farm families. Land has been reclaimed, wells drilled, irrigation expanded, seeds improved; equipment has been sent in for farms; fertilizers and insecticides have been provided. A sum of

$2 million was invested in Greek fish ponds, and these are now bringing in $6 million worth of fish a year.

In Iran, 60,000 chicks donated by American farmers have been distributed by FAO through villages. Fifty purebred cattle have been distributed through Iran for breeding purposes, to develop a strain that will give more milk and more meat. An improved variety of wheat which yielded 25 per cent above other varieties has been developed there by FAO. One hundred tons of this variety of wheat have been distributed among the farmers for planting.

Betel nut is a mild stimulant, probably harmless, chewed all over Asia. The betel nut trees of Iran had nearly all been killed by insect pests. By the help of technical cooperation, new trees have been planted, and these trees sprayed to kill the pests. Pollen was collected from the very few male trees that had not died, and this was spread by airplane in order to fertilize the female trees. This cost two cents a tree, and was paid by the grateful tree-owners themselves. Last fall, a crop worth $450,000 was produced from 50,000 trees.

Into Nepal FAO has introduced five hundred varieties of grains and grasses, legumes and vegetables which it brought from thirty-three different countries. Crops in Nepal probably will be increased 20 per cent by introducing these better plants.

A survey taken by the *New York Times,* published in May 1954, shows that such efforts as these in seventy-nine nations are helping to win the battle against famine.

There has been an increase in food production of 5 million tons in India, and now India announces that she is nearly self-supporting. In Italy there were a million more tons of wheat raised in 1953 than under the brightest days of Mussolini. In Greece, they have raised enough wheat to take care of themselves. Turkey has become one of the four highest wheat-exporting countries of the world. Jamaica is becoming self-sufficient, raising enough rice to feed herself, and Panama now has a surplus of rice, enough to export.

In Korea, FAO's fight to produce more food has kept alive millions of people who otherwise probably would have starved. Experts from twenty-seven nations are in Korea representing FAO. They are teaching the Koreans how to dig peat for fuel, how to dredge harbors, and a hundred other arts. A financial expert from Thailand is advising the bank of Korea. An American veterinarian has taught Koreans new methods of vaccine and serum production. He stopped hog cholera in its tracks after it had killed 43,000 Korean pigs in one year! Korean engineers and American experts are helping to re-establish a great hydro-electric plant which was damaged during the war.

This is but the beginning of the saga of FAO in Ceylon, Turkey, Indonesia, Japan, Laos, Malaya, and Cambodia.

UNESCO

Our next organ of compassion is called UNESCO for short. Its whole name is United Nations Educational, Scientific, and Cultural Organization. UNESCO was established in November of 1946. Today its budget is nearly $10 million a year. Its chief task is searching for valuable knowledge, and spreading that knowledge wherever it will aid mankind. It studies what causes wars, since that is the world's chief threat. Its constitution begins: *"Since wars begin in the minds of men, it is in the minds of men that the defenses of peace must be constructed."* So UNESCO is trying to plant peace in men's minds.

Since UNESCO aims to make all knowledge of the world available wherever it is needed, it is interested in all education and in all schools, from the first steps in literacy to the highest university courses. Since spreading knowledge is its task, UNESCO studies the press and radio, books, television, movies, lectures, art—every channel to the minds of men—and that includes the home.

It undertakes special research in literacy, since three-fifths of the world's adults are unable to read and write. They must be taught to read and write before they can progress far. Otherwise, their progress soon drags to a stop. But teaching half the world to read in the ordinary expensive, slow, painful way requires far more money than backward nations possess.

So UNESCO is conducting a series of experiments with cheaper, swifter methods. As these are tested, results are passed on to many countries. Two large teacher training schools have been opened for literacy and basic education. One is in Patzcuaro, Mexico, where experts are trained in fundamental education for all Latin America. The other is at Sirs al Layyan, Egypt, sixty miles north of Cairo, where experts are trained in fundamental education for the Near East.

UNESCO is also working on the highly important matter of providing much more good material for new literates to read. For the only value of reading is to get *good* ideas. Reading which spreads bad ideas is a curse. UNESCO is alert to this fact, and is pressing for the preparation of wholesome reading matter. A new program of literature production started in Latin America in 1957. Writers must be inspired and trained, for this type of writing is a highly technical skill. What they write must be interesting, helpful, and clear, or it will not be read by those who need it most of all.

Getting the material published, and then getting it distributed where it is needed are equally important. In all this, UNESCO is trying to pioneer.

UNESCO is promoting the idea of universal education for children. Education for all children is a definite policy in the United States and some other lands, but it is far, far from being a policy in most of the world. To achieve this goal of universal education for children, schools must be free, and they must be compulsory. UNESCO cannot of course compel any country to adopt this policy, but it does hold conferences in various parts of the world to promote primary education.

In 1949, UNESCO undertook to standardize Braille for blind people throughout the world. This was especially needed for blind musicians, who want to use the best music of all the world.

The subjects investigated by UNESCO are widely diversified. It is studying desert countries, asking how they can be made to produce more crops. This sounds so much like the work of the Food and Agriculture Organization that the reader may well ask why UNESCO is making this study. Here is the distinction: UNESCO seeks to discover new truth. When a new truth about *agriculture* has been discovered, then FAO will spread it over the world. UNESCO's work is research. FAO's job is putting discoveries to work.

UNESCO finds that many arid zones have very fertile soil which can be used if the areas can be supplied with water, from dams and irrigation canals, or if the water can be preserved from evaporating by the use of reservoirs or vegetation, or if subsurface water can be pumped to the surface, or if sea water can be cheaply de-salted. UNESCO is also studying the winds and the energy of the sun as sources of power to pump water to arid regions.

UNESCO is studying plants like eucalyptus trees, which grow in the desert and provide shade and fuel. Deserts are like infected sores—they spread. So UNESCO is doing research on how to prevent deserts from encroaching on fertile lands. Camels, goats, rabbits, and birds destroy the trees and grasses on the edges of deserts, and then the winds blow the desert sands over cultivated fields. The immense Tigris area was once able to feed 30 million human beings. Now it is a desert. Can it be restored?

UNESCO is studying erosion, seeking the way to protect soil against rains which every year wash millions of tons of good earth toward the sea. It is studying periodic droughts which can convert fertile soils into dust, and the control of insects and parasites which every year destroy at least 10 per cent of the world's food crop, enough to nourish the whole population of Africa or North America!

UNESCO is also studying how to improve agriculture in very cold climates. About one-fifth of the earth's surface is too cold to produce much food. But scientists have discovered that the earth's temperature is now in a rising cycle. The ice is retreating toward the poles. A little more of Greenland (which ought to be called "Whiteland") becomes green each decade. Every year new soil, varying from a few dozen yards to several miles, is being reclaimed and planted in the cold regions of Canada and Siberia.

UNESCO is studying the peaceful uses of atomic energy. The people of the whole world will be able to make vast improvements in their food and in their way of life when atomic energy is used for industrial purposes. Dr. Powell of Bristol University, Nobel Prize winner, declared recently: "Used for production, the power of five hydrogen bombs could furnish a quantity of energy equal to that now produced by the work of *all Britain's miners during one year.*"

All these subjects, and multitudes of others like them, come legitimately under the research programs of UNESCO, which is the *scientific* branch of the United Nations. For these researches it is setting up Research Stations to solve such diverse and sometimes surprising problems as these: keeping high waves out of Madras harbor, finding out how high mud dams may safely be built, how to make it rain in Pakistan, how to protect areas from earthquakes.

One of the most surprising and important services of UNESCO is re-educating the poor but proud white-collar students in many countries so that they will be willing to get their hands dirty at honest labor.

UNESCO aims to build a bridge from the privileged, educated classes to that half of the people of our world who are ignorant and wretchedly poor, and to inspire all men with the hopes and ideals of a better world. This is very necessary if both sides of the world are going to work together. A major part of UNESCO's work is to inculcate ideas of peaceful cooperation. It is seeking to bring nations together in a world community of understanding and friendship, and to teach ideas of racial rights and equality.

UNESCO's educational program covers more than just schools and colleges, as it also publishes international journals to disseminate knowledge, maintains headquarters for the distribution of scientific material and information, provides fellowships so that capable persons may study abroad, conducts international seminars to spread new knowledge, assists in organizing model public libraries. In 1953, when UNESCO opened public libraries in India, 700,000 persons visited those libraries, and borrowed a thousand books a day!

The accusation that UNESCO is "red" is a fallacy. In fact, *no communist country has ever cooperated with UNESCO.*

UNESCO does more than research. It undertakes projects of rebuilding backward areas. In 1948, UNESCO started such a project in the Marvial Valley of Haiti. Twenty thousand people there were ill with malaria and yaws and were starving. The first things they needed were food, quinine and penicillin. UNESCO gave them these.

The history of Haiti is a tragic one. There were two million Indian inhabitants when Columbus arrived, but within a few decades the Indians were almost all exterminated. Then African slaves were brought from the Gold Coast to take their places as laborers. The French exploited Haiti until 1803, when a great patriot, Toussaint L'Ouverture, led them to freedom. Nobody in Haiti had any technical know-how, so the country has been the victim of its own ignorance and of the hostility of its neighbor, Santo Domingo. Three million Negroes are crowded into Marvial Valley, which has the most mountainous and least fertile land in Haiti.

When UNESCO came to Haiti, it built a road into this Marvial Valley, and engineers drilled wells for drinking water. They sprayed DDT in the breeding places of mosquitoes, and built latrine pits to fight hookworm. They put up big posters which said, "Support UNESCO hard." Thanks to UNESCO and the United States, Haiti has emerged from her long history of exploitation and has begun the tedious climb to a new self-respect and a better life.

So ends our story of the United Nations and its subsidiaries.

Paderewski, in Carnegie Hall, at the close of World War I, declared: "We shall save the world not with passion, but with COMpassion." The world's largest instrument of compassion today is the United Nations, with its magnificent programs for children, health, food, labor and research.

CHAPTER 16

THE DECLARATION OF HUMAN RIGHTS

ON DECEMBER 10, 1948, AS MIDNIGHT WAS APPROACHING, THE GENeral Assembly of the United Nations voted to adopt the Declaration of Human Rights. They had labored two years to reach an agreement.

Fifty-six governments voted, none abstaining, and they all voted for it!

They made speeches as they voted, all expressing their conviction that what was being done was of immense significance. They said that this document would be ranked with the Magna Carta of 1215, the Habeas Corpus of 1679, the Bill of Rights of 1689, the American Declaration of Independence of 1776, the French Declaration of Man in 1789, as a landmark in the struggle for human rights and freedom. Carlos Romulo of the Philippines said: "To the roll of historic declarations of the rights of man, the United Nations now add the most comprehensive of all, the first in history to define from a truly universal standpoint the basic rights and fundamental freedoms to which all men everywhere are entitled."

All of these famous documents, from 1215 to 1948, revealed the spiritual level which men had reached in the countries where